Advance Praise

I read Danna's writing with excitement because I know that, in her reflections, I will find some of my own truths. I find myself thinking that we are so different from each other. After all, we are of different ages, races, sexual orientations, religions, family structures. Yet, I consistently find connection to her thoughts and feelings. Her writing is honest, passionate, and filled with wisdom.

Valerie Dorsey Allen, DSW, LSW
Director, African-American Resource Center
University of Pennsylvania

Dr. Bodenheimer writes not only about "how to" for social workers but also talks about the role of the social workers themselves. This emphasis on self reflection is often missing from treatment manuals.

Sean Erreger, LCSW
Stuck on Social Work Blog

Dr. Bodenheimer's book offers pearls of wisdom that all clinical social workers, ranging from novices to seasoned practitioners, can truly benefit from. I plan to include this book as recommended reading on the Advanced Social Work Practice [and] Leadership and Management course syllabi that I teach.

Jack B. Lewis, DSW, LCSW
Assistant Professor
Stockton University MSW Program

On Clinical Social Work

Meditations and Truths From the Field

Danna R. Bodenheimer

Foreword by Jonathan B. Singer

Harrisburg, Pennsylvania

On Clinical Social Work
Meditations and Truths
From the Field

Danna R. Bodenheimer

Published by:

PRESS

Post Office Box 5390
Harrisburg, PA 17110-0390 U.S.A.
717-238-3787 (voice)
717-238-2090 (fax)

http://www.socialworker.com

The New Social Worker Press is an imprint of White Hat Communications.

Text and images © 2017 by Danna R. Bodenheimer

Library of Congress Cataloging-in-Publication Data

Names: Bodenheimer, Danna R., author.

Title: On clinical social work : meditations and truths from the field / Danna R. Bodenheimer ; foreword by Jonathan B. Singer.

Description: Harrisburg, Pennsylvania. : New Social Worker Press, [2017] | Includes bibliographical references.

Identifiers: LCCN 2017021183| ISBN 9781929109654 (pbk.) | ISBN 9781929109661 (hardcover)

Subjects: LCSH: Social service. | Social case work. | Psychiatric social work. | Clinical sociology.

Classification: LCC HV40 .B5456 2017 | DDC 362.2/0425–dc23

LC record available at https://lccn.loc.gov/2017021183

Contents

PART 4: Our Clinical-Internal Worlds

PART 5: On Theory

PART 6: Self-Care

PART 7: What To Do and How To Do It: The World of
Assessment and Intervention

List of Photographs

Foreword

Congratulations. You're about to read a book full of inspiration, hard truths, and passion. This book will give you a glimpse into the world of Dr. Danna Bodenheimer, LCSW, master therapist, educator, and supervisor.

I've had the pleasure of knowing Danna for nearly a decade. I had the honor to interview her about her first book, *Real World Clinical Social Work*, for Episode 99 of the Social Work Podcast. She addressed issues that are ever present in the minds of clinical social workers but rarely addressed in graduate training programs or continuing education, such as what it means to love your clients and how to pay the bills. Episode 99 is one of the most commented upon and downloaded episodes, because people connected with her honest and simple message. As I said in the introduction to the episode, "Clinical social workers will give Danna a high five for so eloquently describing the essence of the clinical social work relationship. Students will jump light years ahead in their understanding of what it takes to become a clinical social worker. Everyone else will get a good sense of the dedication that Danna brings to her work and her writing" (Singer, 2015).

Danna's message comes across as powerfully in writing as it does when she speaks. Danna pays attention to life's details with a psychotherapist's insight and writes about them with the passion of a slam poet. She speaks to the soul of social work and inspires us to think about more than just social work. I'm not surprised that the articles she published on the Real World Clinical Social Work blog on *The New Social Worker* website have been shared by thousands of people.

I re-read several of her blog posts as I wrote this foreword, and I was struck by how routinely readers would write some variation of "this is the best thing I've ever read in all my years as a social worker." For example, when she writes about the perennial topic of the micro/macro divide, she makes the simple yet eloquent point that the economy is a social justice issue AND a clinical issue (see page 216 or *http://www.socialworker.com/feature-articles/real-world-clinical-sw/ when-everything-hurts/)*. It makes no sense to think of the economy only as macro, or to consider our client's financial situation detached from longstanding economic policies. Is this a new insight? No. Do we need to be reminded of it? Absolutely. Danna reminds us of simple truths without sounding preachy or hackneyed.

The photographs in this volume are a gift. Danna's photographs are our window into what it must be like to be in her therapy office. Imagine the story of a client's life is zooming by and Danna sees one beautiful moment. She stops time. She focuses her lens. She sees the ordinary for what it can be: extraordinary, heartbreaking, inspiring, and magical. She frames it and hands it back to her clients. Their moment. Seen through the eyes of an artist.

In one of her captions, Danna reminds us that there is a specific time of day when the light is magical. She talks about taking photographs in magical light, but I think this book is its own version of magical light. Life does not afford us the luxury of seeing our clients and our careers only in magical light. But each chapter in this book is like a ray of magical light that helps us see what is most important about this calling we call social work.

Yes, you've made a wise choice picking up this book.

Jonathan B. Singer, Ph.D., LCSW
Associate Professor, Loyola University Chicago
Founder and host, Social Work Podcast

Acknowledgments

This book is for every student and supervisee that I have ever worked with. I feel enlivened, daily, by witnessing the transition of social work students from the womb of school into the world of the field. The way students and supervisees have brought their cases to life, for me, keeps me engaged and thinking obsessively about the next best intervention and the very best way to think of what is occurring in the clinical dyad.

This book is for my team at the Walnut Psychotherapy Center. You are such a deep and abiding part of me and I love all of you.

This book is for Linda. You are a writer's dream editor and I am so lucky that we met one cold day at a Harrisburg rest stop. You are an unrelenting social work warrior, and you make me feel connected to my own voice.

This book is for Jonathan. The tireless effort he makes toward creating accessible and relevant content for social workers, through his podcast, is a wonder. As is his friendship.

This book is for Jennifer, always Jennifer.

This book is for my children, Nate and Levi. And this book is for my best friend and wife, Kira. You are my light, in any dark, on any day. You are funny, cute, sweet, and my ultimate coziness.

Granular

I basically have two muses—the Hamptons where I spent my childhood and Philadelphia. I feel as if I have studied the beaches of the Hamptons from every angle, in both my waking and dream lives. But I have recently started to study the fact that each grain of sand seems to have a story if you study it closely enough.

Introduction to the Essays

When I think about writing for social workers, I typically think about my social work students or new social workers. I can't exactly explain why this is, except to say that it is my sincere belief that the future of social work lies in our newest members. As political strife and polarity deepen and the disenfranchisement of marginalized populations grows, Darla Spence Coffey (President and CEO of the Council on Social Work Education) reminds us, in a recent message to CSWE members, that "we were made for this."

What Coffey means, of course, is that social workers were built to assess problems, make meaning of those problems, create sustainable solutions, and think with utter creativity and grace. The newest members of the social work community are uniquely energized by untainted energy, a breadth of theoretical tools, and the wisdom of predecessors to enter this world and lift up communities. This book is largely dedicated to you, the new social workers. And you are as new as you feel you are—it is a subjective term, of course. Every time the political landscape changes, I feel like a new social worker. Every time I hear a case from a new perspective, I also feel like a new social worker. Our newness is our passion for social justice and clinical kindness.

I wrote this book over a year's time. I spent one week on each short section. The sections emerged out of what was happening in the world that week, what I saw in a client's eyes, and what questions my students were asking. The sections came together in themes and are organized accordingly. It is a love letter, in many ways, to the field. It is also an effort to have an authentic conversation amongst ourselves about what social work life is candidly like. This is a book that seeks to demystify and honor complexity. It is a book that, above all, is trying to tell the truth. I hope it resonates for you. Before you go on to the chapters, though, here is my first love letter.

Why I Believe New Social Workers Are a Gift

Some clients come in looking for an experienced social worker, and I get that. We are so seduced by the idea of experience. With experience comes wisdom, mastery, efficiency. But we rarely reflect on what comes with newness, enthusiasm, and a recent infusion of education. We rarely hear about clients who come in and ask for the newest social worker. That's too bad because, to me, new social workers are a gift. And I want to welcome you, insofar as that is my job, to the field of social work. I also want to say how lucky we are to have you.

> We rarely hear about clients who come in and ask for the newest social worker. That's too bad because, to me, new social workers are a gift.

In 1970, Kenneth Fisher wrote in *The Iconoclast's Notebook* comparing inexperienced therapists to more experienced ones:

> *Is it not sadly true that the more precision and confidence an expert achieves as to his work, the less he has to say that is particularly interesting? His drive to teach others may increase but, consolidating what he knows, he begins to repeat himself; in a word, having become an authority, he is now seldom inventive. Conversely, if still bewildered and anxious, uncertain as to what the truth is, or even if there is such, perforce he must experiment. He cannot let his ignorance alone. Just possibly he might evolve something that has not yet been spoken.* (1970, p. 56)

There is so much to celebrate in this quote, but mostly I just wanted to share it, because it truly captures the transformative power that your raw talent currently holds. With this quote in mind, here are some reasons why I think clients and agencies are lucky to have a new social worker.

1. You are excited for every appointment or meeting.

I remember clearly feeling a rush of excitement before every new session I had at my new job as a new graduate. I would pour over the paperwork, mentally preparing for the entrance of my client. I would think developmentally, diagnostically, and about attachment in advance of nearly all my meetings. I would anticipate patterns and prepare myself accordingly. Although I still do this, it is much less conscious and more integrated. I don't savor all of this in the ways that I used to. The way it lacks effort for me now takes away from a certain intentionality that I brought to treatment.

2. It is important to you that your clients like you.

Some say it is problematic to want your clients to like you too much. I think that in some ways it probably is, but it isn't that problematic. I hear senior clinicians talk about their cases in ways that can feel devoid of attachment, affection, and presence of mind. There is a way in which senior clinicians stop trying to impress their clients. But what this means is that they are taking their treatment relationships for granted and not working as hard to secure the attachments. As a new social worker, you are seeking the positive reinforcement of having clients return. That means you are working hard to make them comfortable and to create dynamics that are therapeutic and supportive. It means that you are thinking about everything to make the possibility of attachment occur.

3. You are not as likely to reduce your clients down to their diagnosis.

I know that, as social workers, we are all urged to think about our clients holistically. However, after a certain amount of time in the field and work in assessment, the powerful sway of diagnosis can take hold. This is partly because diagnosis serves as a shared language at our agencies. It is also because diagnosis gives us credibility when working in interdisciplinary teams. But when you are first meeting new clients, you will just see them for who they are. I still have my first client, who I met on my first day at my first job. It is now 11 years past that time, but I know that my initial openness to see her complexity set the stage for the sustainability of our relationship. Had she walked into anyone else's office that day, I think she would have been quickly labeled as manipulative, suicidal, and having "borderline tendencies." And perhaps those labels would have been true. But to me, she was my new client and I was only going to see her in multiple dimensions. In fact, I loved her for just being my first, and I think that still holds true. That kind of energy and passion for our work, for the idiosyncratic way in which each of our clients functions, is hard to sustain over time.

4. You are still in the throes of thinking about the role of social justice in our work.

There are few settings that look more closely at the overlap between social work and social justice than academic institutions. Whether you just took your last semester class on racism or you recently learned about the history of social movements, the awakening energy of social justice is pulsing through you. That is awesome. It can fade, and problematically so. The presence of your social justice ear lens keeps your agencies honest. It also grounds your understanding of your clients in the socio-economic context that they need. The more you remain aware of the systems that imprison your clients, the more you see them as full humans worthy of more in their lives. After many years of agency work, we can start to dis-habituate to the ways in which clients are oppressed. It starts to feel as commonplace as the air we breathe and, therefore, keeps us from more clearly seeing the ways that marginalization and social stratification lead to suffering.

5. You read.

I am not saying that there are any social workers that don't read. I am saying that as recent students, you are in the habit of reading. You are also the person at your agency who has most likely read the most recent research, literature, and thought on any given topic. By having had a password to academic journals over the past two (or more) years, you have information that is vibrant and evolving. Share this information. Share it with your colleagues, and share it with your clients. I recently read a paper by a student who had the same supervisor who had supervised me, more than a decade ago. Reading the student's description of what the supervisor said, it was the same theory and advice that I got exactly 10 years ago. I imagine this has to do with the supervisor not having read what is currently being written, or only reading the authors and writers who honor the well-worn pathways that already exist in our minds. You don't have those well-worn pathways. You are willing to read and consider something new, and you aren't married to a particular school of thought. The freedom with which you are dwelling in the material produced by our field will enable your clients to dwell more freely in their own minds, too.

6. Your friends are fellow social work graduates, and you hang out together.

I cannot stress enough the dual importance of a social work social support network and the ways in which this network can fade over time. The more I hear about my students going out together, the happier I am for their clients. This is because I know you are all talking about social work and supporting each other and complaining about student loans and salaries and bad supervision. The more you have social supports to help you negotiate all of this, the more likely you are to be able to be present for your clients. This level of social support is something that seems to be highly present in the years right after graduation and in more advanced clinicians who have time to create societies that they can connect with. Relish this support and know that you are a better social worker because of it.

7. You are in supervision!

First, I am hoping this assumption is true. Second, I am hoping that if you are in supervision, you are finding ways to make the supervision work for you. If you are in supervision, your clients are lucky. I am not saying that every supervisory experience is allowing you to grow, but the simple fact that there is a space dedicated to making sense of your clinical work is a gift to your clients. You are largely working with clients who are so desperate for attachment and resources. Few, if any, people are giving them any thought throughout the week. By being in supervision, you are starting to correct the pattern of their erasure from the world. Without even saying a word about the fact that you are talking about them in supervision, this fact will somehow be communicated to them, giving them both life and breath.

Go out there and know that your freshness is what will infuse essential energy into the minds of your clients and your agencies alike. I am so glad you are here!

Golden Hour

This picture is taken of rowers on the Schuylkill River. They, of course, are concentrating on staying perfectly in sync—a mesmerizing fact of rowing. But the light that reflects from them evokes complete serenity.

Introduction to the Photos

When I started to take pictures, I had no idea where it would take me. I knew that I had long been struck by the idea of stark juxtaposition. Driving through the streets of Philadelphia, many of which have been ravaged by poverty, and seeing the beauty that grows among it, has long captivated me. I have marveled at the idea that a stunning garden sprouts next to abandoned homes, that a nursing mama cat can keep her kittens safe in a box of trashed cardboard, that birds fly proud no matter what is below them. In fact, it wasn't until I started to study and use photography that I realized why there are even birds on a wire. They all line up because they use the heat from the electricity of our power grid to warm themselves. It wasn't until I started to use photography as a form of meditation that I started to notice a lot of things.

As it turns out, for me, photography is all metaphor. And it is largely a metaphor about clinical work. I am not great at it, and I revel in my mediocrity. The same is true for my understanding of my clinical self. I am as good as I can be, but an hour a week with someone can never truly bring their outside lives to us. The fact is that it is almost impossible to be great at photography or clinical work, because nothing can truly capture the temporality or complexity of real life.

Photography, like a session, is just a curation of life, but it does a lot, too. First, it lets you focus on the micro elements of things that we pass by every day because of the sheer velocity of our lives. Someone can talk about how it feels to get on a scale for weeks on end, and we can discuss with them every psychological machination of an experience that probably lasts five seconds at the most. Just as a picture can force us to focus on the details of something that we would likely miss, a session highlights the texture of inner life in a new light.

I think about photography all the time. I think about how I can look at a picture of a bridge taken by a thousand different photographers, and in each picture, the bridge looks different. The power of idiosyncratic perspective is astonishing to me. The power of angle, position, time of day, light—all of it reminds us that, clinically, we should be worshipping at the altar of subjectivity. Without surrendering to subjectivity, we are in a clinical war searching for objectivity, which cannot ever be achieved. Photography celebrates this as clinical social work keeps railing against it with growing pressure to perform evidence-based practices. The more we can engage in noticing the limits and strengths of our own perspective, the more we can understand the limits and strengths of our clinical capacity, and the more deeply our work can grow.

By studying the physical world around me, some notions have become evident to me. First, the stiller the water, the better the picture. This means that if we can find an inner calm, we can better reflect and precisely honor the world around us. Second, I used to dislike Christmas. As a Jewish person, I felt left out. But photography has helped me to invite in the efforts of others to create peace and beauty in their lives. There are few times of the year when this is truer than at Christmas. Many try to turn their homes into inviting art at this time. And, I have chosen to honor the art that others create, which most try to create to survive their own lives, by photographing it.

Finally, I have learned that when you take a picture—meaning the exact time of day—is the whole game. There is a tender hour called the "golden hour" or "magic hour," which is the best time to photograph. Some movies only film during this time, and some photographers will only take pictures during this time of day. Broad daylight can be unbearably stark, and the dark of night can be unbearably dimming. This feels like a clinical reality. There are moments when it works, and they are few, far between, and worthy of chasing. Some call it chasing light. I call it chasing vulnerability. We need to know what circumstances make this light possible and carefully study these circumstances to truly showcase the beauty of our clients' pain and bear witness to the beauty of this pain with them.

PART 1

The Field and Its
Stressors and Realities

No Libs Art

This picture uses a classic technique called "frame within a frame." It is an easy way of bringing in multiple elements. In this picture, there is so much available because of the fact of living in the city. The juxtaposition of an innocently beautiful piece of street art, the steel squares, and the green leaves reminds us of the complexity of each moment, each snapshot that is available to us.

1. Keeping the Clinical in Social Work

It is not uncommon for social workers to feel excluded from conversations on clinical work. There is a misperception that a privileged few are practicing clinically, while the majority of social workers are in non-clinical settings, doing non-clinical work. These misperceptions are rooted in a fantasy of the inflexibility and non-transferable nature of what makes social work *clinical*. The fact is that clinical social work happens everywhere. It is only dependent on a mindset, not an actual physical setting.

There are six key ways in which any social work becomes clinical. These are not anything inaccessible or particularly difficult to construct. Instead, they are simply ways of thinking that shift our work into a transformative and therapeutic psychological space.

1. Manifest vs. latent content

Conversations are made therapeutic or clinical by the social worker's dual attention to both the manifest and latent content. While the age-old proverb goes, *sometimes a cigar is just a cigar,* clinical social work requires us to wonder about what else a cigar might be. This does not mean that we think classically about cigars and simply interpret them as phallic symbols. Instead, we wonder why someone would smoke a cigar and what might be getting in the way of stopping. We wonder about underlying patterns of self-destruction or the significance of the smoking ritual itself. To render social work clinical, we listen for *more,* and think about what is behind the scenes of what is said. The stage itself is considered to be the manifest content, and everything that goes on behind the scenes is considered to be the latent content—the more unsayable and unknowable material. Bringing this material into consciousness is a clinical act.

2. Transference vs. countertransference

In any clinical encounter, there ought to be a willingness to consider the role of transference and countertransference. Transference means the experience of past relationships that a client has had and the impact those connections are having on the treatment. Countertransference signifies the associations and past experiences that the social worker has had that come to the surface as a result of each idiosyncratic clinical interaction. The reason transference and countertransference are of prime importance is that they help us to better under what is happening in any relationship. For example, if an afterschool program is available to students through Big Brothers/Big Sisters and one kid simply won't attend the meetings, it makes sense to wonder if transference is playing a role. Perhaps that kid has been disappointed by an interaction with Big Brothers/Big Sisters before. Perhaps that kid has lost a sibling, and even the name of the organization is triggering.

In regard to countertransference, we need to be aware of our own past and the role it plays in our work, for our work to truly be considered clinical. There are some clients we become inexplicably attached to and others that we simply dislike or would like to avoid. This is typically the byproduct of some sort of countertransferential response. Certain clients elicit different responses in us. This phenomenon is almost always associated with the unconscious ways we are bringing our past relationships and stories to the table.

3. Symbolic symptomology

Although we have to take symptoms seriously and largely at face value, we also need to consider the deeper meaning of symptoms. We see clients who are actively symptomatic all the time. We might have a client who is actively having auditory hallucinations or engaged in compulsive rituals. We need to think about how to reduce the symptoms *and* how to understand them. In clinical work, we are in the relentless business of meaning making. This meaning making ought to accompany our efforts to alleviate the symptoms.

Why does someone engage in compulsive rituals? Often, it is to create a sense of internal equilibrium and safety. If we are advocating for symptom reduction, via medication for example, we can think about ways of enhancing internal and external feelings of safety. Thinking about symptom meaning and symptom reduction is a dualistic way of thinking. It is also a clinical technique. The more levels that we think on, the more clinical our work becomes, regardless of our setting or intervention.

4. The past makes itself known in the present

Yes, an awareness of one's past can take the shape of studying transference. It can also simply happen through a studied attention to which parts of an interaction are about the *here* and *now* and which parts feel like psychological residue. For example, if a client is repeatedly late for meetings or never properly fills out the paperwork for additional services, we need to wonder if this is resistance about something in the moment or a way to work out unresolved struggles from the past. Noting that every interaction is laced with historical remnants strengthens our capacity to help clients toward the future. It is our willingness to see behaviors as multi-significant, and aiding our clients to do the same, that can liberate them from the shackles of imprisoning past struggles. Sometimes the mere utterance of the distinction between past and present can induce change and create transformational liberation.

5. Attachment style

Although I am not of the mind that attachment style is performed or experienced unilaterally, I do think that attention to attachment tendencies renders our work more clinical. People generally tend to attach in three separate ways: *securely, anxiously,* and *avoidantly.* Their attachment style is relevant if they are on an oncology floor in a hospital, or if they are in a com-

> **The fact is that clinical social work happens everywhere. It is only dependent on a mindset, not an actual physical setting.**

munity mental health setting. It is a lens through which to understand clients and the ways in which they are interfacing with the world. Attachment theory suggests that we are all biologically driven by attachment. But our past attachment experiences influence how we interact in the present and have diluted, many times, this biological drive. Many of our clients have created internal defensive structures to regulate their disappointment and fear around attachment. This often results in confounding behaviors, across settings, which are better managed by being better identified and understood.

6. The whole person

Finally, our work is made clinical when we refuse to divide a person up according to their diagnosis, past behaviors, current behaviors, socioeconomic realities, racial identity, job status, sexuality, and so forth. This is the hallmark of our profession—it separates us from other similar fields, and it renders almost everything we do as clinical. This is because recognizing the whole person heals the whole person. Accustomed to systems that isolate parts of the self and interact with only these selected parts, a person can become re-integrated by our willingness to mirror the magnitude of their individual complexity.

Social work *is* clinical social work. And clinical work, done well, is infused with social work values that create several restorative possibilities. The clinical social work values should be used in diverse settings that don't readily identify themselves as clinical, but are in fact profoundly and exactly that.

2. Negotiating Salary, Negotiating Worth

To me, salary is a social work issue. The fact that many of us graduate making less than we were making before graduate school is a travesty. Wrapping up classes in May invariably results in dialogue, panic, and questions around salary. These are some of the most important conversations that we can have with each other. Further, the more transparently we discuss salary and financial stress, the more we can shift away from the paradigm that suggests that social workers ought not make decent money.

Many students and rising graduates ask me what is a fair salary to expect. This is the wrong question. The first question we need to ask ourselves is: *How much do we need to live on?* This is not a simple question, and it requires some significant research into our own lives. Instead of saying, *I want a salary of around 40K*, we need to say the number that represents our actual living expenses. Our living expenses ought to cover necessities, pleasures, and savings. I am not saying this to sound unrealistic. I am saying this because we need to be clear about our needs.

As social workers, we have an inherent tendency to underestimate our own financial needs. This is a huge mistake. Once you agree to a salary, you agree to a way of life for at least a year, with only incremental change to follow. Our problematic solution to this problem is to add jobs, hours, and stress to our lives, rather than better assessing our needs at the outset of salary negotiations. I have seen people estimate their living expenses negating their awareness for the need for food, let alone the life sustaining need for self-care.

So, start with an honest and—hopefully—overestimated budget of your life. You can be aspirational. You can be honest. But please don't downplay the need to live with some air to breathe. Then go to an online salary calculator and put in the number. Put in the number of what you need to take home, not what your salary offer says. If you want to make 40K in Pennsylvania, that means you will be netting $21,654 with no dependents. That is $1,804 per month. Student loans will take up a lot of that. So will rent, food, parking, gas. So, is 40K enough? I don't know. The answer depends on the facts of your life. It should not depend on the facts of an individual agency. There are a million salary calculators online.

When you get an offer, you must counter it with the actual number you have determined that you need to live on. If there is a discrepancy between that and what the agency then comes back with, ask what it would take and how long until you will reach your number. This isn't strategy—there is nothing to be shy about. This is the amount of money it takes to finance

> **To me, salary is a social work issue.**

your life, and you need to be able to talk openly and honestly about that with people who offer you a job. You should offer total transparency, and you should expect the same in return. You are not asking for much. I know this, because you are a social worker. And if you were asking for "much," that wouldn't be the worst thing. You are about to do the hardest work of your life, and you should be remunerated for it.

Here are some questions to ask when you are talking salary:

- Is my position grant-funded? If so, how much of the grant is going to salary? How is that determined? Was it by the grantee or the agency? What is the length of the grant? What happens when the grant is no longer funded?

- How was my salary determined? Is it according to level of education or licensure? How can I expect my salary to grow in the next five years?

- Is there anything that I can do at the agency that would enhance the amount of money the agency makes and therefore increase my salary?

- Would it be possible for me to have flexible hours, so I can supplement my salary with other work?

- Because my salary does not cover my student loans, does this agency have a student loan forgiveness program? Is this an agency that the government considers qualifying for student loan forgiveness?

- In addition to my salary, would it be possible for you to cover my supervision that would help me achieve the next level of licensure? (This is typically a tax deduction for agencies. It is not hard for them to offer you this.)

- Can I have a clear sense of what advancement looks like at this agency? What potential can I realistically achieve working here?

Of course, these are some broad questions. But they are also questions that demonstrate your knowledge of how agencies work, how salaries are determined, and of your intentions for securing your future.

I once had a supervisee who was in a grant-funded position but didn't understand the nuances of this reality. At the end of the grant year, the grant needed to be used fully, and she was required to organize an "event" for her clients. The event cost around $4,000. Could this money have been better spent on her salary? I have no idea. I know it would have helped her life. I also know that it is okay to ask about numbers, to learn about numbers, and to talk openly about these things. Needing a salary is not something to be ashamed of. And, being agreeable about whatever you are offered is not an act of good will; it is an act of complicity.

Oftentimes, salaries are determined by a sensation about what a social worker "should" be paid, based on local standards and expectations. It is through an activism that is structured by a self-awareness of our professional worth that these local standards can change. These standards are based on a false folklore about an expected martyrdom by our field. They keep us painfully stuck and disempowered. This harms us, and it harms our clients. Asking for more is the only way forward.

3. On Social Work Supervision

Given that it is impossible to advance one's level of licensure without substantial supervision, the import of the subject of supervision is inarguable. Despite this reality, discussions on what constitutes "good" supervision are scant, at best. This is largely because the pressure of managed care and decreased agency funding has led many to use supervision as a space for the management of administrative tasks, reflecting the powerful scarcity of time and resources. The multiple pressures on all social workers has forced dedicated clinical supervision to fall by the wayside. Thus, supervision has lost its sacred standing in our field.

Although there might be a dwindling focus on the essential nature of supervision, that does not change the sheer necessity of it. For supervisors and supervisees alike, the need to honor the supervision process is vital. Supervision is the underlying life force that keeps our field ethical, evolving, and intentional. Supervision ought to be where wisdom is shared, clinical voices are cultivated, and cases are conceptualized.

Given this inarguable level of import, let's talk about what makes supervision good and what makes supervision bad. I say it that plainly because there is a lot of good supervision that happens. There is also a lot of mediocre supervision that happens, and that is a fact that must be examined.

Mediocre supervision

Let's start with the mediocre. Mediocre supervision is, first and foremost, co-created. The forces that underlie mediocre supervision are intricately intertwined. There is the over-burdened supervisor, the chaotic agency setting, and the supervisee who is inhibited about clearly articulating needs. No one wants supervision to become mediocre, but it is hard to keep it alive. Pressures for precise paperwork, audits by insurance companies, and high caseloads leave supervisors depleted and supervision deadened. This deadening leads to supervision that is largely superficial, thereby neglecting the depth of the clinical work. Amidst this depletion and deadening, supervisees tend to put their needs aside in the hopes of making everyone's job easier, avoiding the obstructive role of the squeaky/needy wheel.

Supervisees often feel pressured to come to supervision prepared with a set of questions to support the efficacy of the meeting. Supervisees also feel responsible for presenting the ways in which they are smoothly adhering to the agency's treatment modality. For example, if an agency strictly practices and bills for trauma focused cognitive behavioral therapy (TF-CBT), then most of the questions will be about how to use this technique and how to get clients to become more responsive to the technique. While preparedness for supervision makes sense, as does adherence to agency modalities, these constructs can render supervision inauthentic and performative. This performativity stunts the growth of both the clinician and the supervisor and leaves the truth and grit of clinical work outside of the supervision room.

Authentic supervision

In clear opposition to this performativity, the very real and rich possibility of authentic (good) supervision remains powerfully possible. Good supervision is a great thing. Our field was largely founded on the power of supervision, identifying it as the site at which practice wisdom was imparted and social work neophytes became social work magicians. Rather than a focus on model adherence or administrative tasks, supervision was a place where the expertise of a seasoned supervisor brought these magicians to life. Of course, this still occurs quite a bit, but not enough.

Good supervision requires openness and vulnerability by the clinician and the supervisor. Many supervisors are legitimately frightened by the weight of the responsibility of supervising. They are essentially taking on the caseload of a younger clinician in the hopes that the clinician is making sound decisions. Every time supervision happens, a license is on the line. This requires a certain bravery that needs to be mutually recognized. However, this bravery cannot be managed through a false sense of authority. Instead, it is the vulnerability of a supervisor that can allow for the transformation of a clinician and, subsequently, for that clinician's clients. For example, a clinician might present a case of a client in a dangerous domestic violence situation. The clinician has almost habituated to the stories of abuse, losing their sense of alarm. The supervisor can come in and offer authentic fear for the client and empathy for the desensitized clinician. This fear and empathy, once transmitted, can allow a social worker to reawaken the client, feeling more fueled by the tender witnessing of a supervisor.

The presence of a supervisor's vulnerability lessens the very real threat of shame for the clinician. Endemic to many supervision dynamics is a simultaneous avoidance and experience of shame. Supervisees often assume that they are being rigorously judged. And, supervisors feel a level of responsibility that can lead them to act authoritatively certain of right from wrong. Rather than remaining entrenched in this polarization, a supervisor's vulnerability invariably lifts this shame and opens up clinicians to more clearly see their own blind spots. This vulnerability also allows supervisees to be open more purely and honestly around their internal processes.

Good supervision requires the steady knowledge of parallel processes. What happens in a supervisee dyad almost always shows up in a clinical dyad. In other words, if there is shame in the supervision, there will be shame in the clinical work. If there is a toleration of vulnerability in the supervision, this will also trickle down. If a supervisee is withholding information from the supervisor, this likely means that clinical information is also being withheld in the treatment. There is no supervisory dynamic that operates in a vacuum, although this is something that is often forgotten in our work to stay afloat in high pressured, high volume settings.

The blur between therapy and supervision

Further, underlying effective supervision, an understanding of the inevitable blur between therapy and supervision must be tolerated. Much of what is brought up in supervision touches on the deepest parts of the clinician who is sharing it. In good supervision, we often bring up what rubs us most intimately. I had a supervisee discussing a client's history of sexual abuse recently. He was brought to tears hearing about the details of the vicious experiences of his client. While I know that he is clearly moved by his client's story, the resonance of the story felt deeper than that. We started to talk about his fears for his own son and the ways in which this client reminds him of his child. If we had only talked about the client, the undue amount of emotion would have remained displaced onto the clinical work. By allowing for the blur between therapy and supervision, we create the possibility of clearer delineations in the actual treatment.

Most social workers feel a decent amount of haunting by the lives and stories of their clients. I have a question that I ask most supervisees: *Which clients are you brushing your teeth with?* It is a strange question, but what I am aiming to discern is which clients are most deeply penetrating the psyches of my supervisees. I ask this question, first to normalize how much we keep our clients with us. I also ask this question because I sincerely believe that the hold our clients have on us is lessened in the presence of supervision. While supervision is not designed to dilute intense clinical relationships, it is intended to create enough psychic space for the supervisee to clearly think.

If a clinical relationship feels like a pressure cooker, supervision is the space where the steam can be let off. The relief of letting out steam is often supported by the supervisor's reminder of theory, attachment patterns, and clear signs of countertransference. The supervisees might be driving with their low lights on; the supervisor helps with finding their brights, too. The internalization of a decent supervisory relationship allows the clinician to create impulse control around the crafting of interventions. Ideally, an intervention comes to mind, and before immediately acting on it, many will take the idea to supervision. Together, a solid choice can be made. The internalization of supervision helps supervisees to feel safer in the decision-making, knowing that there is a clear space for them to carefully consider their options, and to reflect on their choices in retrospect.

The messiness and the magic

Supervision requires a certain messiness to be effective. In supervision, clinicians are asked to look within to better understand their role in their clinical efforts. Deepened self-knowledge can only occur in the presence of a safe and non-judgmental relationship. It is also reasonable for supervisees to demonstrate fears about not having any idea what they are doing. A large part of the supervisor's job is to help clinicians develop language to better identify their own thinking and clinical choices. A clinician might say, "I had no idea what to say, so I just sat there." A supervisor can healthfully respond by saying, "It sounds like you were working to tolerate the silence your client needed." Supervisees need to be able to give voice to their terror around incompetence and inefficacy. Supervisors can tolerate and normalize these fears, while helping clinicians to find their own voice, wisdom, magic.

There is certainly no one right way to do supervision or to be in supervision. But consistent, carved out time for supervision that happens reliably is central to the growth of any social worker. Further, good supervision ought to be crafted to tolerate ambiguity and confusion, allowing a social worker to ultimately find the way toward ethical, curative, and theory-based interventions.

Yes, administrative tasks and crafted agencies are a valuable use of supervisory time. But it is worth considering that these agendas are often attended to as a defense against the mutual vulnerability it takes to engage in transformative supervision. Good, great, not mediocre, supervision can transform a supervisor, a supervisee, and their clients.

4. Scapegoats and the Social Work Workplace

At the agency where I am in charge, I recently hired someone who had been fired from her last job. A few people asked me if I had known that she was fired, and I said, "Absolutely." There are times when people are fired because they have a poor work ethic or have made compromised and problematic choices. There are also times, many in fact, when people are fired because they have become their agency's scapegoat. These employees, in my experience, are often brave risk takers who have taken the fall for complex organization dynamics. Furthermore, social workers often take the fall for larger issues in interdisciplinary settings because of our low ranking on the overall professional totem pole.

Let's start with the original story of the scapegoat. The scapegoat, as an archetype, is mentioned everywhere from the Bible to Greek mythology. While there are variations on how the story is told, the basic summary is that an animal is used to represent the sins of the community. The animal was typically a goat. Members of the community would go to the goat and confess their sins. When the ritual was over, the goat would be sent into exile, cleansing the community of its wrongdoings. The term *scapegoat* has come to mean the person in the system who bears the blame and burden, unfairly, for others.

There are several ways in which the scapegoat gets chosen, unconsciously. First, perhaps the scapegoat is quite outspoken and is vulnerable to giving voice to the issues that no one else wants to. In taking this risk, it is easy to become targeted, because of perceptions that are established around this person's already existing role. When the blame shifts to this specific target, no one is particularly surprised or suspicious.

Second, members of racial groups that already bear the brunt of significant misperception are more apt to fall prey to the part of the scapegoat. It is not uncommon in group settings that have disproportionate representations of diversity for the minority group member to become scapegoated by complex unconscious processes.

Further, in settings where social workers do not have a lot of power, but do have a lot of responsibility, the possibility of becoming scapegoated increases significantly. This becomes even more true when the level of responsibility that the social worker holds is untenable and unrealistic. When we are unable to achieve the tasks in front of us, we often become scapegoated, rather than better supported to do our jobs.

There are central pieces of the scapegoating process that are worth keeping in mind, particularly as it relates to social work. Scapegoating removes us from one of our central ethical constructs, which is to see everything as part of a whole. When someone is scapegoated, we are denying this conceptualization in the service of identifying an easy target. Further, scapegoating can only occur when we turn a blind eye to complex power dynamics. It is our work, when someone is scapegoated, to try to unearth what structures are at play that have made the simplistic blame game possible.

The following are some of the underlying reasons why scapegoating might occur.

Complex grant funding structures. Many of us work in jobs that are funded by grants. These jobs are either funded philanthropically or by state and government entities. For funding to continue, of course, proof of progress must be consistently reported. To secure a grant, agencies often promise more than they can deliver. Furthermore, grants typically have indirect reporting structures, meaning that the social worker with feet on the ground is not typically the person reporting directly to the funder. When the funder is disappointed or the funds are threatened, it is almost always the social worker who is doing the direct service who gets blamed, in the interest of preserving the relationships of the people above them.

Salaries, assumptions, power dynamics. Other agencies or organizations, like hospitals or medical settings, for example, rely on social workers to complete the work of both assessment and discharge. The work that is done in between is considered the work of the utmost importance. This is true of surgery, giving out antibiotics, and psychiatric prescriptions. Because so much of the work that falls outside of social work is considered more important, our value is established as relatively "less" than those around us. There is a saying, often used in work places, that goes: "the last one in is the first one out." While social workers might not be the last ones in, they are paid the least (frequently). Our work can be considered dispensable. Therefore, when something doesn't go well, overall, we tend to be the first one out, or the first one blamed. Furthermore, we keep such a tremendous amount of information in our heads, our processes are so unknown to the disciplines around us, that the depth of our work can be danger-ously underestimated. Think, for example, of what occurs when there is a death of a child in the care of Human Services. Often, the mayor or governor will demand an explanation from the head of Human Ser-vices, and the head of Human Services will serve up a social worker as the part of the system that failed. Rather than looking at the overall system, we are often the ones to take the fall.

We tell difficult truths. As social workers, we are imbued with the responsibility to act as social change agents. This often means that we see unacceptable dynamics around us, dynamics that fall short of anything that could be considered socially just. When we see these dynamics or failures, we give voice to them. In doing this, and often revealing what those around us don't want to hear, we risk becom-ing scapegoated. While there is sometimes reward for acting as the squeaky wheel, there is also tremendous professional risk associated with it.

Here are some ways to han-dle scapegoating.

Pay attention: If you are not the scapegoat, but someone around you is, don't feel relieved. The fact that scapegoating is possible at all in a social service agency means that it can happen to you. There is little safety in a setting that unevenly distributes blame. It is important to study this dynamic and to be wary of it, rather than to take comfort in having nearly dodged it.

> **If you have been scapegoated, it is worth knowing that this might be a result of your social work strength and tenacity, not your weakness or inefficacy.**

Enlightened witnesses: Alice Miller, author of *The Drama of the Gift-ed Child* (1981), describes the essential role that enlightened witness-es play in group processes. Enlightened witnesses are colleagues and social work peers who bear witness to the complexity of our work, are eager to understand our processes, and can stand up for us when oth-ers cannot see our strengths clearly. Having an enlightened witness can either prevent the possibility of being scapegoated or can aid in our efforts to make sense of being scapegoated when it occurs. Either way, these partners in work can make a huge psychological difference.

Reviews: People are far more susceptible to scapegoating when they are not being reviewed on a regular basis. When we are not clear about how we are doing and there is no formal review structure, we are far more vulnerable to sudden shifts in perception and leadership moods. The more we are kept in the loop about our performance and the better documented our reviews are, the more control we have over surprising dynamics at work.

Structural transparency: It is always essential to have a clear sense of how the structure at your workplace functions. For example, if you are in a grant funded position, you should collect information about the funder. The more you know, the more potential you have to avert being blindsided by opaque modes of communication.

Preparing yourself and studying scapegoating dynamics is both empowering and a social work value. It is our work to see complex systemic functioning, which scapegoating almost always renders reductive. And if you have been scapegoated, it is worth knowing that this might be a result of your social work strength and tenacity, not your weakness or inefficacy.

Beach Glass

My love of beach glass isn't original. It is a common adoration. However, what I love most about beach glass is photographing it. Sure, I savor running my fingers over the softened edges of the weakened points of glass. But I also love studying the juxtaposition of the colors of glass against the colors of nature. Sometimes the glass highlights nature and sometimes it mocks it. This seems like an enduring truth of the battle between industry and nature.

5. What's So Wrong With Social Work School?

Don't get me wrong, I love social work. I even loved social work school. I've been around the block a time or two after having attended two social work schools (one for my master's and the other for my doctorate) and teaching at four. Through these experiences, I have gotten a clear sense of some of the factors that might be compromising your education or leaving you with a feeling that you didn't graduate with a sense that your education was enough. I am offering these reflections with the hope that they are validating. I am also offering these reflections with accompanying suggestions that might make your education feel more worthwhile, even after you have graduated.

The curriculum is just too generalist.

One of the most difficult aspects of master's level social work education is that it is typically only two years long. Of course, this is also a strength. It means that you don't pay for more than two years of school, and it means you get into the field quickly. However, it also leaves your classes lacking the depth that many of you are hoping for. To me, many classes felt like survey courses, jumping from topic to topic every week—one week on CBT, the next on DBT. You just aren't ready to practice CBT after learning about it for one week. Of course, you might be lucky enough to take an elective, but finding a diverse set of electives is increasingly uncommon with budget cuts at most universities and colleges. Even in second-year practice, arguably your most advanced class, the sense that there is not time to delve into any one topic looms largely.

Furthermore, it can feel as if the classes are not in proper order. You take Human Behavior in the Social Environment before you are in placements that render it applicable. When you need that theory most, you are already a year past the material and don't know exactly how to integrate it. There is something about the way the classes are ordered that makes theory integration and case conceptualization particularly challenging. It goes beyond simply having HBSE the first year. It also has to do with the emphasis on research (which is heavily supported by the Council on Social Work Education) and the ways that those classes often cut into clinical material (if that is what you are most interested in studying). Given that you only have two years in school, it is painfully difficult to be spending time in classes that don't feel supportive of your overall goal of becoming a clinical social worker (which is what I am emphasizing here, given that this is the topic of this book). For macro students, these issues might not apply in the same exact way.

Suggestions

- Do everything you can to get undergrad research classes to count toward your MSW research classes, freeing you up to take more of what you want.

- Decide in advance what it is that *you* want to know more about. Seek out the professors who know about this, gear your papers toward it, read about it. Don't hesitate to use your time in school in a way that is specifically tailored toward your needs.

- Keep your notes from your first year on hand during your second year, to support your effort to integrate complex pieces of material into your educational experience.

- Pursue electives, pursue electives, pursue electives. Some students can't fit electives into their schedules or don't feel the selection of electives is adequate. Then fight for more, and do everything you can to make the schedule work for you.

We talk about race and oppression, but we don't integrate it.

Everyone has taken some kind of class on race, multiculturalism, or diversity. These courses go by different names—too many to count. Some schools offer these classes at the beginning of your education, and others close out with them. I feel that these courses are inarguably essential. My problem with them lies in a few different areas.

First, it seems that we often limit our discussion about difference to topics of race and class. There are few other places in the curriculum, unfortunately, that address issues of intersectionality. We rarely have the time and space to talk about sexuality and race, disability and race, disability and sexuality. Of course, we are intensely focused on issues of racial oppression in social work, and we should be. But delving more deeply into how difference presents itself, even talking about racial oppression, often seems to fall short.

Second, it is very difficult to bring the topic of racial oppression and racial differences into the classroom process. Discussions about race often take place in a highly intellectualized, if not defended, manner—leaving the dynamics in the classroom off the table. Often the dynamics in the classroom symbolize some sort of historical racial enactment that is worthy of discussing in the moment. Historically, we are undeniably in a heated moment, and keeping this fact and the liveliness of it outside of the classroom can lead to feelings of frustration and disenfranchisement.

And perhaps most frustratingly, the topics of race and oppression rarely make it into our other classes. Because there is a class designated for this topic, it is almost as if the topic exists in a vacuum separate from our other studies and work. These topics need to be integrated into the overall curriculum, rather than leaving them to be dealt with separately and on their own.

Suggestions

• Ask all of your professors, particularly those in your core classes, how issues of diversity will be covered.

• Google pictures of the authors of the articles in your syllabi (throughout your classes), and assess whether you are truly reading materials from diverse voices. I have found that the majority of reading materials are by White writers (in the core classes), and the diversity in the syllabus only shows up in some electives or classes specifically designated to address difference.

• Ask how difference in your placements can be productively discussed in your practice classes. These classes are the place where you ought to be able to "practice" the most difficult skills that you are cultivating. Negotiating complex and intersecting differences ought to be addressed in practice during both of your school years.

Adjunct vs. standing faculty

The power imbalance between adjunct and standing faculty is not unique to schools of social work. More and more schools rely on adjunct faculty to teach their most essential courses, while standing faculty make fewer and fewer appearances across the curriculum. For social work, this can be amazing. The reason is that adjunct faculty are typically in the field, and you need this. You need faculty who are connected to what is happening out there. To become tenured at many colleges and universities, standing faculty need to abandon the field in the service of research and service to the university community.

For you, the problem becomes that adjunct faculty (who might be excellent or might be horrible) are totally influenced by a system that results in inherent job insecurity. They are aware of course evalua-tions and often teach in fear of them. They are also handed a syllabus that they have very little control over or investment in. Most adjunct faculty have no real connection to the school, no office space, and very little time to grade and correspond with you. Given the amount of practice wisdom that adjunct faculty have, the fact that you often don't have increased access to them is disappointing and frustrating. Further, many of them function on a short leash that creates a real struggle when it comes to bringing their whole selves to the class-room.

Suggestions

- Try to take classes that are taught by both adjunct and full-time professors. The diversity helps. You should be able to be exposed to professors who are deeply invested in your school and professors who are currently working in the field.

- Ask your adjunct professors how they are balancing their field and teaching lives. There is a lot of wisdom to be gained from this kind of multitasking.

- Ask standing faculty what they are researching and writing. Often, reading what your professors are writing will enrich your academic experience tremendously.

- Asking standing faculty if they need any help with their re-search will also serve you very well in the future, particularly when it comes to recommendations.

- Approach every social work class you take strategically. As-sessing your professors' relationship with the school will aid you in this process.

Overall

Getting your MSW is no cakewalk. It is a complicated process that can feel rushed and underdeveloped. At the same time, it goes so quickly that it can be hard to know just how much you are learning. And you are learning a lot!

Here are some overall suggestions to help you make the VERY most of it all:

- Every social work professor, on some level, is well intentioned and wants to create excellent social workers. They might be tired, stretched too thin, or preoccupied with other issues at the school. But, trust me, they are there for you. The more engaged you are, the more engaged your professors will be.

- Trust the process. It can be almost impossible to even know what is happening to you in the middle of it all, but you are being transformed by this education even though you might not even know how or why.

- Ask for what you want every chance you get. Without students, schools don't exist. Use your voice, knowing that you are driving the school. You are the customer of the business, and on some level, the customer is always right.

- Be creative in forming relationships. The relationships you form in graduate school might truly last you for your whole career.

- AND, use your supervisor as an ally, as a professor, as a friend. Being a supervisor is an honor, even if it is a burden, too. Know that so much of your education takes place in the field. There is no more crucial player than your supervisor. Your keen usage of this relationship will reward you in spades.

6. Social Work Ethics in the Real World

For most of us, our social work education begins with an introduction to the NASW *Code of Ethics*. The fact is that we all need to come up with our own set of guiding principles, as well. The *Code of Ethics* is an excellent set of guidelines, but increased clinical experience forces us to more clearly articulate a set of ethical standards that inform our clinical interactions and decision-making processes.

Over time, I have found tremendous comfort in the NASW *Code of Ethics*. I have also come to some additional conclusions about how to practice ethically. These ethical guidelines have been born of work with a highly diverse caseload across multiple practice settings.

Context

What differentiates our field from parallel disciplines is our commitment to understanding the system within which our clients function. What this means in practice can vary. It can mean that we understand socioeconomic oppression prior to subscribing to diagnosis. It can also mean that we rarely see an individual's functionality as distinct from the family system that they are embedded in. For me, thinking from a systems perspective has come to mean that I pay attention to the everyday context of our world. For example, issues of racial injustice have dominated our social discourse in recent years. The vitriol of the 2016 presidential campaign was inarguably pervasive. When thinking about client functioning, I have come to think of the system they live within, in addition to the moment by moment impact of pulse and environment in our lives. Clients often disavow or are unaware of how the background noise of our world is affecting their psyches. It is our work to help our clients to understand that we are living in times that truly brutalize the psyche and that it is worth understanding how we can become triggered and how we can work to protect ourselves.

God

The NASW *Code of Ethics* calls on us to have utmost respect for diversity. We often think about sexuality, gender, and race when discussing diversity. And although religious diversity is named, we don't study the significance of this as closely in our training. I have come to find that, ethically, I will believe in whatever God my client believes in while we are meeting with each other. This may seem odd, but the fact is that to truly join clients in their journey, I surrender fully to their belief system while we are together. I find that this allows me to stop judging, questioning, or wondering about if there is a God or not. It also allows me to stop wondering if a client is using religion defensively or dysfunctionally. Instead, through a surrender, I am able to enter my client's world, which has invariably led to richer clinical work.

Absurdity

To work in better accordance with social justice values, the notion that social inequity has reached absurdist levels is worthy of serious consideration. The old adage, "If you aren't outraged, you aren't paying attention," is of particular import. The income gap between men and women, White people and Black people, gentrified vs. non-gentrified neighborhoods, is absurd. While there are systemic issues that we ought to pay attention to in order to understand why things are the way they are, this should not alleviate the level of outrage that we feel about it. I have found that if I am able to hold the outrage for my clients, it provides them with some relief from having to hold it all themselves. I have also found that my clients feel supported by my understanding of how systemic oppression is affecting their lives. Part of our underlying clinical work must be to keep a steady eye on the increasing ways in which oppression traumatizes the psyche. Our psyches become traumatized when meaning cannot be made of pain. The level of inequity, at this point, completely lacks justifiable meaning, thereby rendering it more psychically dangerous. Recognizing and holding this truth is a clinical imperative and ethic.

Identity

While there is great attention paid to the importance of valuing diversity in the NASW *Code of Ethics,* less attention is paid to the fluidity of identity. Awareness has grown around the fluidity of gender identity. However, fluidity around all aspects of identity is a valuable clinical ethic. It is very difficult to not become attached to seeming facts about our clients. In fact, we even introduce our clients with their demographic information. For example, I might present a client by saying: *My client is a White, 31-year-old, heterosexual woman who is Christian.* The problem with this is that these stated "facts" become ideas that I am now attached to in order to orient myself to my client. However, subscribing to the possibility that many of these identities are fluid allows our clients more space to grow, change, and evolve. I have a client who has converted, religiously, two times. I have another who has moved between multiple gender identities. This becomes difficult for me when I feel as if I know something about my client for sure. Instead, I am coming to try to orient myself to my clients' need to change and grow, knowing that there are very few places in their lives where alternating identity presentations are possible.

Supervision

I am confident in the essential need for supervision in social work. We ought to use supervision to help us with our blind spots. We also need to use it to keep ourselves boundaried and clear. We ought to use it to support our case conceptualizations. However, part of our social work mandate is to also recognize when *not* to use supervision.

Not everything our supervisors say is true or right. We need to find ways to use social work supervision honestly and openly, but not with complete deference. Our social work mandate, instead, is to hold onto ourselves and to develop our own clinical voices, taking supervision into consideration, while gut-checking our own values and making our choices in accordance with what feels most true to us. We inevitably know our clients best, and nothing can substitute for this truth.

Meta positions

One of the most difficult social work challenges is to occupy multiple psychological spaces while working with our clients. We need to be close to our clients, listening to their stories, hearing their questions, noting their attachment styles. We also need to be hovering above the treatment, making sense of what is happening in a larger way, identifying patterns, tracking symptoms, and studying defenses. We need to be in the real relationship, while also making sense of powerful transference and countertransference trends. A social work ethic is to become someone who straddles multiple ways of being at the same time. We can easily fall into one role or the other, only studying our client or only being with our client. However, our work is only truly made clinical and potentially curative if we are to hover between worlds and spaces. It may seem strange to consider this an ethic, but at the same time, if our role becomes oversimplified or two-dimensional, we are not fully serving the complexity of our responsibilities.

7. Quit Your Social Work Job

Let me be clear—not all social workers should quit their jobs. In fact, some of you are at perfectly stimulating and meaningful jobs. And some of you aren't. Most of us have a somewhat conflicted relationship with our jobs. This is mostly because the ways in which we work in America are inherently burdensome and overwhelming. Despite the normalcy of this reality, some of you are working in jobs that are not sustainable, and it might be time to wonder about what is next for you.

The question, for many of us, is: *How do we know when it is time to quit a job?* Although I don't know the idiosyncrasies of your personal situation, I wanted to share some thoughts on what might make a job unmanageable for you to continue.

Sundays don't help.

Almost every social work job will leave you somewhat breathless and depleted by the end of the work week. This is just the nature of our work and, for the most part, it is a good thing. Our days are dynamic, we are always faced with something new, and we simply run out of steam. But the weekends should replenish us and leave us feeling ready for Monday. If your anxiety and discomfort in your job leave you squandering away all that Sunday has to offer because you are dreading the week so powerfully, this is of significant concern. It makes sense to need a refill of breathing room, but it does not make sense if the breathing room that you have is filled with fear.

You are triangulated with a bureaucracy that leaves you powerless.

For almost any social worker to have direct access to clients, there is some sort of governing body involved. This may be the administration of your agency, or it might be insurance companies. It could be a board of directors or a principal of a school. Of course, the intention of these governing bodies ought to be that clinical work is occurring in a safe, ethical, and evidence-based manner. But we all know that things don't always play out this way. Often, our work with clients becomes diluted by our need to manage whatever the governing party is at our agency. While this is commonplace, the concern grows when we are unable to serve our clients properly. We seize our capacity to properly serve clients when paperwork demands more of our time than we can handle, when treatment becomes overly prescriptive and rote because of its manualization, or when we find that we are simply not treating our clients in a way that feels ethical. This can happen in a school setting when we are asked to act as operators of discipline or in a hospital when we know that we are discharging someone with insufficient resources. When you are in the position of feeling as if your clients' needs are not able to be your priority, it is time to question how to proceed.

You wish you had never gone to school.

When all of us started social work school, it was with the intention of somehow changing the world for the better. As social change agents, we fantasized that the relationships we formed with others would serve as the basis of their transformation and ideally the transformation of their communities, too. And while there is a lot of loftiness in these ideals, you spent a lot of money on how to refine your skills to honor them. If you feel that these intentions have become mere afterthoughts, you need to consider your professional environment. It is unequivocally true that great clinical work can offer transformation and relief, if not to communities, certainly to individuals and families. If this has come to feel impossibly true to you, it might be worth examining the role your agency is playing in your shifting beliefs. Social workers ought to be perfect hybrids of realism and optimism. But operating in only one of these spheres will make you inarguably disappointed and perhaps resentful of the very important investment that you made in your own future.

You just can't pay the bills.

We all know that social worker salaries leave something to be desired. This is perhaps the most stressful aspect of our work. We pour our hearts into it, but our bank accounts rarely reflect this reality. Doing this work, however, when our level of financial strain preoccupies us constantly, diminishes our efforts. If, at the end of every month, you wonder how you just survived or fear that one of your services is going to be cut off, I would say this is an unmanageable level of stress. If you find that you are always ignoring phone calls from debt collectors, this also falls under the heading of unmanageable stress. Your boss needs to know how you are struggling, because it is almost impossible to keep producing under these circumstances. It is also impossible to attend to self-care under these circumstances.

Your empathy is gone.

The single greatest clinical tool that we have is the provision of empathy. While we don't have to love or even like many of our clients, we do need to be able to access their subjective experiences and feel something for them. This offering, this intervention, is ultimately the breeding ground for most psychological growth and change. There are a lot of reasons why we find ourselves running low on empathy. The reasons might be personal or professional. It might be that we have just seen the same thing over and over. It might be that we aren't getting adequate supervision and we have no place to discharge everything that we are feeling. If you feel that you are running out of empathy, it is essential to determine why. If it is because there is something inherently numbing about how you are working or what is expected of you, this is worthy of serious reconsideration.

But when and how?

We have certainly all heard the "rule" that you need to be at a job for at least a year before looking for another, because job hopping looks "bad." The year rule is a myth if you are applying for a job while still working at another. Simply being employed makes you a more attractive candidate. Perhaps the length of time you have been at a job is a factor in hiring, but it isn't the only one. Experience, level of licensure, and good references all outweigh it.

Furthermore, agencies understand that the field has shortcomings that can lead to burnout. This is something you can be honest about. Moving to a new job in the hopes of having renewed energy is not something to be ashamed of. It means that you are committed to the sustainability of your career and the quality of your clients' lives.

8. Leaping Into Private Practice

You may be considering starting a private practice, but you don't know if the time is right. It might be worth talking through this a bit. And given that I have a lot of experience with this whole thing, I thought that I might be able to help you.

You can do this.

There are many different private practices. There are full-time and part-time practices. There are practices with evening hours or weekend hours. There is no reason to think of a private practice as an all-or-nothing scenario. One of the best parts of starting a private practice is that you can take it slowly. You can rent an office full time or for just a few hours a week. If you are ambivalent, I think it is worth finding out how it feels by giving it a shot. The investment, which I will talk about, isn't so high that it should be prohibitive.

It is important to do this.

There is a lot of criticism around private practice—particularly that private practices don't properly serve underserved communities. The fact is, though, that there is something radical about helping clients on your own terms in a space where you have brought your own version of safety. In most agency settings, there is a certain amount of triangulation that dilutes direct client-to-clinician contact. Cutting out the significant complications that this reality brings can deepen the work. There are ways to provide incredibly affordable treatment that might make private practice work more accessible. For example, in my practice, we have a group in which everyone pays full fee. This allows us to offer a group to lower-income clients for $1-$5 per meeting. The notion of inaccessibility can be remedied with sufficient creativity and forethought.

Furthermore, the financial transactions that private practice requires are of terrific import. I don't know why, but starting to establish a set of fees and asking for money forces us to deal with some of the most intrapsychic issues that we have. It brings to the surface our old wounds and patterns of functioning. The facing and, ideally, resolution of these issues strengthens us clinically.

We are also forcing our clients' hands by asking for money. The fact of this transactional dynamic lends itself to healthier boundaries, a more solid clinical frame, and the psychological resonance of money in the lives of our clients. Money is a legitimate and essential realm of clinical fodder, and bringing it directly into the relationship allows for the closer examination of its complex role.

Everyone has a niche.

Many suggest that they are unable to start a private practice because they don't have an area of specialization. This feeling of not being able to properly describe your own practice can feel prohibitive. First, it is important to note that some people claim an area of specialization that is based on nothing more than a conference they attended or some CEUs that they collected. Others, more authentically, claim an area of specialization because their experience does run deep. But having a niche is just a way of branding. The fact is that no two clients are the same, and even if you have an expertise, it will not prepare you for what you will see hour after hour. So, suffer the feeling of having a false sense of self in order to brand yourself. Then let your false sense of self get repaired by the truly complex and idiosyncratic work you will do.

Marketing is cheaper than ever.

One of the central reasons why starting a practice can feel overwhelming is the expectation that associated expenses will be too high. But the advent of social media as a marketing tool has substantially leveled the playing field. In the practice that I run, *all* of our marketing has taken place using Facebook. We didn't even need to use Twitter or Instagram. There are many Facebook groups that you can make use of to market yourself. For example, if your area of specialization is eating disorders or infertility, chances are there are local Facebook groups for people

> Starting your own business, big or small, is scary, and it should be. But that doesn't mean it is wrong or that you are unprepared.

who identify with these issues. There is trust and buy-in within these groups, and they serve as resources that can create the possibility of word-of-mouth and reputation building.

Others use Instagram or Twitter to brand themselves.

These communication tools allow you to create a voice for yourself in ways that therapists have never had the capacity to do before. You can share articles, write pieces of your own, and build up a dialogue with your targeted treatment community. And for the most part, it is all free.

There is no lack.

The mantra "there is no lack" is one I repeat to myself over and over again. What this means, basically, is that there is no lack of resources to go around. There are enough clients, there is enough money, and there is enough healing. The work we do is too essential to underestimate. And, it is my strong conviction that the need for excellent clinical social workers in practice is more powerful than ever. The need for therapy is both timeless and timely. There is enough work to go around. So, whatever mantra you need to keep reminding you of this, claim it!

Mastering *Psychology Today*

When building a private practice, *Psychology Today* will be your best friend. You need a *Psychology Today* ad to have any credibility. This is where most people go to find and verify the credentials of a new therapist. It is useful to assess your market using *Psychology Today,* as well. If you do a search for your area of specialization with your intended ZIP code and five pages of therapists come up, it will be hard to get clients. If you find a ZIP code very nearby, in a neighborhood that is not as saturated, you have a better chance of coming up in a search and getting phone calls.

Writing your *Psychology Today* profile is an art unto itself. It is helpful to have as many friends as possible read your ad, basically crowdsourcing responses to it.

End of paperwork

The fact is that there is very little paperwork involved in starting a private practice. You need your social work license, your malpractice insurance (which shouldn't cost more than $200 a year), a criminal background check, and a child abuse clearance.

All of your other paperwork should be web-based. There are many software programs available. I certainly don't know about all of them, but have heard that both *Simple Practice* and *Theranest* are user-friendly and intuitive. If you are going to take insurance, these programs interface with insurance companies and simplify the cumbersome reality of those processes.

And the cost of them, of course, is tax deductible!

Leap of faith

Whenever you start a private practice, it will be a leap of faith. There is no level of preparation that will allow you to dodge this fact. Although planning is essential, because you can start slowly, there is a fair amount of learning that takes place as you go. There are people who spend months creating a website. Others launch it and tweak it as they go. There is no right way to do this; many different styles work. What doesn't work is preparing to the point of paralysis.

Starting your own business, big or small, is scary, and it should be. But that doesn't mean it is wrong or that you are unprepared. I have heard many people speak to the feeling that they will feel as if they are throwing a party and no one will come. I have felt this way myself. However, every fear that comes up when building a practice is emblematic of a larger life theme. Trying to avoid facing these life themes only gives them a more powerful hold over our lives.

Reluctant Companions

My older dog, Annie, is the love of my life. I don't discuss her age, because I don't like to deal with it. We got a puppy suddenly one day, and there was no clear reason why. I knew that Annie wouldn't be happy about it, but that she might accept Clover (the puppy) as part of our pack. It turns out that dogs, like people, are ultimately driven more by attachment and body heat than anything else. They reluctantly seek comfort in each other while acting like it isn't happening. The background wall art says it all, of course.

PART 2
Attachment and Trauma

9. Twin Traumas

Following the attacks of September 11, 2001, there was a tremendous amount of literature written about the impact of having a shared trauma in clinical dyads (Coates, Rosenthal, & Schechter, 2003; Pierce, 2006; Tosone, Bettman, Minami, & Jasperson, 2010). It was an amazing clinical moment, because the shared vulnerability of the therapist and client, alike, was crystal clear. It also became totally acceptable for the therapist to not be more evolved in negotiating trauma than the client. For a moment, we were all admittedly in the confusion, rage, fear, and sadness together.

What feels so stunning about the passing of that moment is that we, clinically, have lost sight of the very real fact that 9/11 was one of many shared traumas that clinicians and clients co-occupy. It was an acceptable issue to discuss at the time, because it was so obvious and so huge, and there was no shame in being affected by it.

I think it is fair to say that we have receded back into the fantastical recesses of believing that our clients are traumatized, while we, their social workers, are not. The power of this false dichotomy pervades our work as we learn about the trauma of our clients, as if we are not talking about ourselves the whole time. Most of the time, our clients have some sort of trauma histories. But the hard truth is that so do we. We, of course, are supposed to be on the side of either not having been traumatized or on the side of having worked through our trauma enough that we are not at risk for feeling triggered or unhinged by our own pasts.

For starters, let me offer a definition of trauma that will help us all to know what I am talking about. The definition of trauma is clearly debatable and complex. To combat that, I am going to use the *Webster's* definition of it, to simplify that part of the discussion. The dictionary defines trauma:

- *an injury (as a wound) to living tissue caused by an extrinsic agent*
- *a disordered psychic or behavioral state resulting from severe mental or emotional stress or physical injury*
- an emotional upset

The broadness of the definition of trauma is useful here, because I am trying to acknowledge the far-reaching impact of trauma. To add to the definition, I will say (in my own words) that trauma usually includes an attack on an attachment, a feeling of being out of control, and a loss of internal and external sites for safety.

We don't know how many people are traumatized. It would be impossible to calculate, not only because of underreporting, but because we don't all fully agree on the definition of it. We do know (at the least) that 1 in 4 college women report having been sexually assaulted in their lifetimes (Perez-Pena, 2015). That number has remained constant since the 1980s. And that is just sexual assault. Given that statistic alone, it makes sense to finally acknowledge that clinicians are often trauma survivors, and we bring this to our treatment.

I write this as a trauma survivor, myself. In a way, I feel inhibited saying that and at the same time, of course, there shouldn't be any surprise there. There are many of us who are trauma survivors, and oftentimes the only thing that separates one trauma survivor from another is the willingness to identify as such.

Okay, so what about all of this? What does it mean if we ourselves are traumatized? Can we still be good at our jobs? How evolved beyond our trauma do we have to be?

I operate with these questions in mind all the time. I think about them as a professor, a therapist, and a supervisor. When I am teaching about trauma, I know my students are trying to learn more about their clients, but are also listening for information to better understand themselves. I see them taking dutiful notes, while I see them internalizing the information to deepen their own understandings of themselves. I know they are hiding this, and I also want them to know that it is okay.

I want you all to know that it is okay that you have been traumatized. I want you to know that it is okay that sometimes you feel triggered and scared and ashamed. I know that you wonder if you can be good at this work when you have been through your own histories, and I know that this question is terrifying.

It is amazing, because in the field of substance abuse, there is shame when the clinician has *not* been through some sort of addiction and come out the other side. Clinicians who are not sober often wonder if they can help their addicted clients. Why is the opposite true for trauma? Why are we often made to feel that if we have been traumatized, we can't help people because we are too messed up? Perhaps the answer has something to do with gender, but I don't think it is that simple. And I am not exactly sure that the answer matters.

What does matter is that the shame transforms into something else, something powerful.

This is what I have come to believe: I am not sure that we can do this work well unless we have gone through some sort of a trauma.

There is something quite magical and painful about the traumatized mind. The traumatized mind is one that is highly sensitive, attuned, and capable of understanding nuance and complexity. It is sensitive because traumatized folks typically have had to study their abusers to try to survive their trauma. This study of psychology was initiated by something horrible, but it was initiated early and has left many of us as experts in our field. It is attuned because those who have been traumatized have typically learned how to tune in to the needs of others to keep themselves safe. This is a complex phenomenon and typically the byproduct of two things. First, for many who have been traumatized, the pain of being in one's own mind can be unbearable, and we have vacated our own mind to be in the mind of another for relief. Second, because we know the pain of trauma so well, we can carefully pick up on it in others.

Some say that those who have survived trauma have antennae. I think this is true. Trauma survivors are capable of understanding complexity and nuance, because many of us know our abusers and simultaneously love and hate them. We know that many emotions can be held at one time, because we have done it ourselves. Ambiguity is something in which we are well versed.

10. I Believe in Ghosts

The more I practice clinical social work, the more I believe in ghosts. I don't mean ghosts in the classic sense. I don't mean apparitions or floating white sheets with two cut-out eyes. Instead, I mean that our work is haunted, on many levels, by relationships and historic interactions from the past. Moments of stuckness, incomprehensibility, and clinical frustration can often be understood when we open our perceptions to the role that the past is playing in the present. Ghosts invariably and subtly inform our work. Considering this possibility can unleash tremendous psychological liberation.

My belief in ghosts is multidimensional. First, I think that the very self-worth and dignity of our field is dictated by ghosts of the past. In almost any clinical team meeting, social workers feel that they are at the bottom of the professional totem pole. This is ironic, given that the knowledge that we have of clinical work holds tremendous nuance and complexity. Strikingly, we are also almost the least paid player at many professional tables. Why? It certainly can't be that our work is of less import. Quite the opposite, really, we offer tremendous cohesion to treatment teams while providing unique relief to struggling clients. Our training and skill set make this specific form of relief possible.

> **Our work is haunted, on many levels, by relationships and historic interactions from the past.**

I don't know exactly why. I have some hypotheses, all related to ghosts. There is the obvious parallel process between the long-standing marginalization of our treatment populations and our professional marginalization. Clearly, systemic, institutional racism and classism have long characterized the functioning of our country. Within this social stratification, social workers remain cast aside, mirroring our clients' fragmented, forgotten, and chaotic lives.

One of our founding and most supportive mothers is certainly Anna Freud, Sigmund's daughter. Anna was Sigmund's last born, sixth child. Before finding out about his wife's pregnancy, Freud had started to speak impassionedly about the essential need for the accessibility of birth control. In this effort, he was talking about his own exhaustion from having kids. Anna wasn't wanted. Perhaps in response to this painful knowledge, she fought hard to make meaning of the child psyche. She used her findings to empower social workers with tools to effectively work with children. The dynamic between Sigmund and Anna is a relic with which we are still wrestling. Social work, perhaps the wise child or counterpart to psychiatry and psychology, often feels like the last child to join the clinical family. Ghosts of the past, felt in the present.

On a more micro level, I often find that working dyadically with a client is misunderstood. The possibility of there ever being just two people in relationship is a psychic myth. In any clinical dynamic, there is both silent and roaring ancestry. This ancestry is present for the social worker and the client, alike. Of course, this can be referred to as transference and countertransference—I like to talk and think about ghosts.

The ghosts are certainly not limited to those who have died, although this is often the case. I had a client recently crying about her pervasive feelings of hopelessness and despair. She just can't seem to find her way out of it. Finally, after many months, we started talking about her sister's death that occurred nearly 15 years ago. She said that she fears that the experience of joy would mean that she has stopped missing her sister. She is being held hostage by the simultaneous disavowal and engagement of her sister's ghost. To do this work well, we need to welcome the ghost, name the ghost, and free her from the ghost by befriending it. Talking to the ghost allows us to invite in the possibility of the ghost's wisdom. Her sister would never have wanted her to be beholden to sadness this way. Refusing to welcome her only propagates the sometimes malignant experience of grief. When, in fact, grief can heal.

Another client is working as a Therapeutic Staff Support (TSS) social worker in a rough inner city school. The student he accompanies through the day is being viciously bullied. As he sees the bully, he feels overcome by insatiable rage and violence. To regulate this ire, he must interact with the ghost he holds of his inner bullied, child self. In recognizing the haunting presence of his own, wounded past, he can begin to properly serve his client. Without recognizing the ghost, his ghost, he is imprisoned by a spirit that cannot distinguish between past and present.

When taking a new job, we invariably battle the ghosts of the past employee and workplace dynamics that existed before us. Researching this history makes us more adept at navigating the pitfalls created by an unresolved era. When working with new clients, it is essential to ask what their experiences with past social workers have been. Why? Because we need to know about the ghosts that preceded us to understand how the present is, often, inexplicably playing out. Learning about how a past employee at our agency has violated boundaries, welcomes a ghost. Hearing that a client has never trusted a social worker before, welcomes a ghost.

Ghosts, certainly, are only scary when we ignore and deny them. The freedom of our present is made possible by peacefully and fearlessly facing our always haunted pasts. The past makes itself known in the present, simply in disguise. Our work, as clinical social workers, is the unrelenting disrobing of the disguises that surround us.

11. Childism and Its Implications

When my son was 18 months old and first started daycare, he came home and mumbled some variation of a saying that has now become very familiar to me, as a parent. In his broken toddler tongue, he said some variation of "You get what you get and you don't get upset." I hadn't heard it before, so I looked into the etiology. It seems that it was the title of a children's book in the 1970s and took hold as a tool for everyone from managers in fast food restaurants to kindergarten teachers. It is a saying intended to help manage disappointment and frustration tolerance. Underneath it, though, is a powerful message to children: *just get over it!*

In 2011, Elisabeth Young-Bruehl, a powerful thinker, professor, and writer, died of a pulmonary embolism while leaving the opera with her partner. Her death viciously disrupted her evolving work on a concept that she called "childism" (Young-Bruehl, 2012). The term was coined to capture the systemic ways in which children are not only discriminated against, but also hated. She, along with Alice Miller, author of *The Drama of the Gifted Child*, argued for the preservation and honoring of the vulnerability of the child psyche. Both eloquently suggested that while, as a society, we believe that children are our precious priority, in fact, the very opposite is enacted.

The idea behind childism is that there is an unconscious pull to invalidate the psychic lives of children. This invalidation happens in both subtle and highly evident ways. Subtly, children are often asked to behave in ways that defy their developmental capacity. There are children who are asked to act as emotional partners to their parents, or children who are asked to parent their younger siblings. There are children who are asked to cook and provide for themselves and children who are asked to go to school sick.

Most of these requests are not born out of malice, but of a society structured in a way that leaves many of us desperate. So many parents are left single and emotionally alone because of violence, prison, and drugs. Others are terrified to take a day off from work, because they are at risk of losing their jobs. The fear that we can't properly attend to our children cuts across socioeconomic lines and leaves most of us making decisions that we know don't serve our children.

Aside from asking our children to step outside of their developmental capacities, we neglect children as we pervasively over-diagnose their childhoods. Whether is it medicating children for "ADHD"-like behaviors or compulsively referring to kids on the spectrum, we have become consumed by the diagnosis of childhood, rather than the diagnosis of society. If children cannot sit still throughout a school day, why are we so quick to assume that the problem lies with them? Why are we even quicker to assume that it is acceptable to medicate a child with medications that largely lack the scientific research supporting their safety? Not all diagnosis is wrong, of course. But certainly, not all of it is right, either.

In Pennsylvania, there were 29,273 reports of suspected child abuse or neglect made in 2014, of which 11%, or 3,340, were substantiated (Pennsylvania Department of Human Services, 2015). Sexual abuse was present in 52% of the substantiated reports. I am not even sure what to make of those numbers. I know that 29,273 people are not paranoid. I also know that there is a tremendous amount of abuse that is sub-threshold for agency involvement, but not sub-threshold in terms of the ways in which the child psyche is affected. I hear, on at least a weekly basis, that something happened in a child's life that they won't "remember." For example, when discussing sleep training and the famous "cry it out" method, we assume that the child won't remember the tears and strain to communicate. In these claims, we systematically deny the very power of preverbal trauma. We know that the infant mind remains imprinted upon, influencing decades of attachment experiences. Yet we cannot fully hold this truth, because children don't have language to describe their inner experience.

But even when the language comes, do we listen? How many children are accused of lying, manipulating, or just seeking attention? I sometimes wonder if children ever do lie, or if we have decided that they are lying because their truths are too unbearable to take. I know that children often wouldn't even have the ideas that they are sharing, if those ideas weren't taken from somewhere, some context clue or exposure to an overstimulating truth.

When Freud first started his studies of hysteria, he diagnosed an epidemic level of childhood sexual abuse. He was aware of the hyper-sexualization of children, but receded into a re-narration of his hypothesis to better please his audience. He changed his original tune to a song of how children were titillated by their own desires, developing sexualities, and shame over their attraction to their parents. Speaking largely to the parents of hysterical children, he opted to protect the adults. Parents, he claimed, could only innocently and stoically stand by as children went through the stages of psychosexual development. But every time we go to Target and see words across the back of a little girl's pants that say "daddy's girl" or "princess," we know that Freud was right the first time.

I wonder about Young-Bruehl's embolism, a death by losing breath. I think that when we immerse ourselves in the depths of childism, all the real and stunning ways that it is enacted and the ways that we are a part of it, it becomes breathtaking. Miller, who spoke passionately about the ways in which children serve the unmet narcissistic needs of their parents refused to back down from her position. Ultimately, she died in 2011 in near isolation but clear on her message.

As social workers, our responsibility is to reveal systemic maltreatment and to then claim our role in the perpetuation of that maltreatment. As with racism and classism, our hands are all dirty. The same is true for childism. Perhaps the understated reality of it is the best evidence of that fact that we have.

It is okay to get upset about what you get. And, we need to allow our children to develop authentic emotional lives that honor their truths, not just ours.

Childhood

While this picture was taken at the perfect time of day for a sunset, it also speaks to some facts of childhood. These are my two boys playing with each other. When they are at the beach, they don't notice the passage of time, as evidenced by the shift of day into night. They also don't ever seem to mind that the water is cold. I am amazed that children are so indifferent to the realities of water temperature when I bristle at every single gradient of it.

12. Troubled Me, Troubled You

There are times in our work, too many to count, when we get into trouble in our personal lives. Sometimes the trouble is of our own making. Sometimes things just happen to us. Perhaps we overdraw our checking account or our mom is sick in the hospital. It is impossible to avoid these swamplands. The question is always: *How can we stay professionally afloat during them?* I wonder about this often, but usually when it is too late and I am merely gasping for air.

A few years ago, I was in a horrible housing predicament, having sold our house before securing a mortgage for a new one. In between sessions, I was leaping toward the phone for updates, obsessed with finding security for my small family. When there was no message or update, I would wonder how I would survive the next 45-minute hour without checking my email every five minutes, if not more. I would sit in session fantasizing about taking my phone and throwing it against the wall and hearing the glass of the iPhone screen shatter. I have no idea why that was my wish. But I couldn't stop imagining it.

Self-care, of course, is always suggested. It can sometimes help us preventatively or as an intervention. But when our internal resources are drained, it is particularly hard to find ways to take good care of ourselves. In fact, I find that it is when I am doing my best that I can be most creative with self-care. During my lows, I can find no way toward it.

I have no clear answers on how to help during these times of trouble, but I will do my best. First, what can feel most crazy-making, while simultaneously practicing and suffering, is the way in which our struggles are made invisible by our clients' naiveté about them. Of course, our clients shouldn't know about our complex personal lives, but that doesn't mean that being unseen feels good. This is why it is essential to have some people in your life who know about what is going on with you. Whether it is your supervisor, close friend, or partner, sharing your suffering keeps your work healthy and boundaried.

This invisibility is often made worse by our own refusal to admit when we are having a hard time. Although there is no clear binary between when things in our life are fine versus when they are not, there are definitive times when we know we are swimming upstream. It is of terrific import to name these times to ourselves. We need to own them and claim them for what they are—an unavoidable aspect of our own humanity. To live in the world honestly is to suffer in it. There is no shame in that. Just because we are social workers does not mean that we have all our stuff figured out. The more we pressure ourselves to feel like we are "okay," the more our suffering takes a toll on our overall wellness.

Pragmatically, there are ways to honor our own struggles. It makes sense to create space between clients. If you are used to seeing clients back-to-back with only 10 or 15 minutes in between, adding just five or 10 minutes to this can shift your ability to recalibrate in dramatic ways. Often, when we think about self-care, it feels like an impossible endeavor. However, small shifts that allow us to check Facebook or Instagram, or call our moms, can return us back to our psychological base.

Beyond the ideal of self-care is the inarguable need for attending to our basic human needs. There is no time when this is easier to abandon than when we are suffering. Attending to our basic needs takes incredible energy and determination. If we don't eat a regular amount, breathe some fresh air, and sleep for around eight hours a night, we are causing ourselves tremendous strife. Furthermore, we are unable to serve our clients. It is okay to be distracted, tired, angry, and anxious. It is not okay to work when you are hungry and debilitatingly exhausted. While this is obvious, I know, it is also a subtle reminder that while self-care can feel like a luxury, attending to our bodies' most basic standards is a necessity that renders our work possible.

I have come to strongly believe in the healing power of one daily practice. I am not referring to something complex, expensive, or inconvenient. I am talking about making an inarguable pact with yourself to do one consistent thing daily. Part of the reason I suggest it is that when this daily practice is something you can't attend to, you can have a way of recognizing how much you are struggling. Think of the daily practice as a thermometer of your wellness that goes off when the daily practice cannot be properly honored.

Finally, while our own struggling depletes us, it can also lend tremendous depth and texture to our work. The goal is not to hide our pain, but to recognize the way that it can serve as clinical connective tissue. This is a way of thinking about use of self. By speaking from the place that knows pain, uncertainty, and suffering, we help transform this in our clients. I am not describing a revealing of content, but a shared affective experience that often lends balm to the lonely wounds inflicted by anguish, fear, and chaos.

13. On the Orlando Mass Shootings and Beyond

There isn't much for me to say about Orlando that hasn't already been said. Most of the debates about the underlying causes of the massacre at the Pulse nightclub have happened somewhere in the media or on Facebook. That said, it seemed irresponsible and avoidant to write about anything else the following week—because, the fact is, even with everything that had already been articulated, we needed to keep talking. And talking and talking and talking. And even though I had no overarching goal in talking about what had happened in Orlando, there were a few points that I wanted to make that I feel were particularly relevant to *us* as clinical social workers. This is what I wrote that week.

This is about mental health and it isn't.

The more wary we are about linking what happened in Orlando to mental health, the better. First, of course, the killer in Orlando had mental health problems. This is simply inarguable. But it is not fair to label him with Bipolar Disorder, which has happened many times so far. People with bipolar disorder don't commit mass murder. This was not the byproduct of a manic episode. Suggesting that it was puts other people with bipolar disorder in danger and vastly overestimates the significance of the disorder. It is certainly possible that he seemed manic during the killing, but that still doesn't mean that we can categorize him as Bipolar. Omar Mateen was clearly a sociopath, something very different from someone with Bipolar Disorder. He completely lacked a moral compass, which is something very unusual for someone with a mental health disorder.

The other reason why linking this to mental health is problematic is that it places some of the blame and responsibility on clinicians. The underlying message when people discuss mental health as a source of mass shootings is that mental health practitioners might have been able to stop it, or should be able to stop it. We can't stop someone like Omar Mateen. One, we don't have the resources. Meeting with a client once a week could never suffice. Neither would two or three sessions a week, which insurance wouldn't cover anyway.

If he had been inpatient, his stay likely could not have surpassed 30 days, let alone five. If anyone wants to discuss the issue of mental health in relationship to Orlando, then insurance companies must be considered at the front and center of that dialogue. I have to defend treatment to insurance companies almost every day. Clinically, we are simply up against a wall.

But most importantly, Omar Mateen didn't seek treatment. Most sociopathic people wouldn't. We can't fix what is not in front of us, which is why the need for better gun control is so essential.

This is about the closet and it isn't.

There is increased chatter about the possibility that Omar Mateen, the killer in Orlando, was gay, perhaps closeted. I still can't quite piece together what is so troubling to me about this narrative, but there are some salient points about it that I would like to make, nonetheless. First, the closet is dangerous. It is a psychologically torturous space to reside in. Often, our bodies beg for us to find release from performing an inauthentic sexuality. That said, this release rarely (if ever) takes the shape of homicide. Instead, most of the pain of a closeted sexuality is turned inward and leads to self-harming and suicidal tendencies.

By definition, sociopathy means that someone lacks a social conscience. To remain in the closet is all about social consciousness. Someone is terrified that their sexuality will threaten their attachments to both family and community. Someone who is sociopathic is disinterested in attachment completely.

BUT, the piece about Mateen's sexuality that does feel worth holding onto is about the very powerful and primitive defense: *projective identification.* Projective identification means that there is a part of ourselves that we utterly hate, despise even. It is a part of ourselves that we feel we must rid ourselves of. Unconsciously, we identify someone who has this trait, or seems vulnerable to having this trait, or has something similar to this trait. We believe, again unconsciously, that if we destroy that person, we will be able to rid ourselves of this very real piece of our identity.

Let's say, for example, that there was a part of George W. Bush that hated his father. Obviously, there are a lot of reasons why this wouldn't feel okay. It is terrifying to hate your parent, particularly when that parent is beloved and as powerful as being the actual president. One way to deal with the hate is to become president yourself, to outdo your actual father. But it is also to identify someone else who hates your father. You then would seek to hate and destroy that person yourself. Saddam Hussein wanted to kill George W. Bush's father. Perhaps by killing Hussein, Bush could rid himself of his own familial hatred.

I am not sure if that sums up the war in Iraq, entirely. That would be a pretty bold hypothesis. On the other hand, I do think that it is worth taking the risk of projective identification that seriously, because it is *that* destructive.

Did Mateen kill 49 people to kill a part of himself? I don't know. Clinically, it is worthy of some consideration.

Macro vs. micro

I feel personally drawn to understanding the events in Orlando through the lens of failed gun policy. I know that there is tremendous work to be done to heighten regulations and to create sensible legislation. But none of that helped me when sitting with clients on Monday morning, following this horrible hate crime and massacre.

> I often feel drawn to macro issues when I don't fully know how to handle the micro experience of overwhelming pain and grief.

I often feel drawn to macro issues when I don't fully know how to handle the micro experience of overwhelming pain and grief. This isn't, of course, to say that macro issues are avoidant. In fact, they are completely essential at this moment. But I am a clinical social worker doing clinical social work. That means that even when I am in the depths of horrible psychological pain, I need to show up and sit with someone for about 45-50 minutes and hold it together. This week, that has been incredibly hard. I imagine it has been hard for many of you, too.

This is what I have learned from it.

- It is okay to not be great at our work every session and every day. Some days greatness is getting through the day.

- Sometimes our clients heal us. I had a straight client ask me, her lesbian therapist, how I was doing. This felt like a gift. I said that I was okay, and I thanked her for asking. It was a one-to two-minute exchange over a lengthier session. But it was just the substance I needed to show up for her.

- We don't need to have the answers, and our clients don't need us to. All our clients need, many times, is someone who

DOESN'T try to make it better. Instead, they need someone to agree that right now things are hard and, hopefully, next week will feel better than this week.

- It can disturb our clients to see that we are fine, when we shouldn't be. We should not always suggest that we are okay in the service of our clients' needs. Sometimes they use us as a measure of how they should feel. When we perform "fine," it can pressure them to do the same.

- Sometimes our clients need to see our politics to feel safer. I don't mean that we need to say who we are voting for or where we volunteer our time. That said, demonstrating our outrage about Orlando is a political act. So is the understanding of what happened as a hate crime. Saying this heals.

What happened in Orlando is partly about Orlando itself.

Of course, I don't blame the city of Orlando for what happened at the Pulse nightclub. However, Florida has a long-standing history of policies that have created a hostile environment for the LGBTQ population. Because, as social workers, we think holistically and systematically, this is worth noting. In Orlando, gay sex was considered a misdemeanor until 2003. It was not legal for gay families to adopt or foster children until 2015. There are no workplace protections for the LGBTQ population, meaning that being outed or out allows management to terminate someone's employment. And perhaps, most dangerously of all, Florida allows doctors to refuse the care of the LGBTQ folks, because it is one of the states that does not protect against medical discrimination based on sexual orientation.

It is worth completely feeling devastated about what happened in Florida. It is *also* worth completely feeling devastated by what *has been* happening in Florida for decades. There is a lot of room for activism and awareness here, and I think it is worth unveiling the many ways to consider our own country's role in the travesty.

Finally, this was a crime about intersectionality.

While this was an attack on the LGBTQ population, it was specifically an attack on the Latino and Latina members of this population. There are perhaps no more vulnerable members of American society than queer people of color. Queer people of color make up huge portions of homelessness in our population, are powerfully and consistently victimized by extreme violence, and often suffer from extreme levels of poverty. Many of the people who were murdered at the Pulse nightclub were working two or three jobs to put themselves through school, to support their families, or to try and create businesses. All their stories—every single one of them—are riveting and symbolic of how marginalization creates struggle. Whether it was a first generation student entering college or a mother of 11, few of the victims of this massacre were doing anything but trying to get by while honoring the complexity and beauty of their identities.

When mourning what happened, let's mourn specifically *and* precisely. Let's recognize the community that lost the most—a community that has fought to be out in ways that we are only beginning to truly comprehend.

14. Poverty as Trauma, Social Work as Cure

In March 2016, the American Academy of Pediatrics declared poverty as the single most pressing, chronic health issue facing children in the U.S. (American Academy of Pediatrics, 2016). In fact, the number of children living in low-income, poor families increased from 39% in 2008 to 44% in 2014. Recent ground-breaking research has shown that poverty is likely the largest determinant of adverse health experiences throughout the lifespan. The lifespan itself is greatly reduced by the presence of poverty, often deep poverty, during early childhood.

A simple questionnaire (see Starecheski, 2015) that assesses the presence of adverse childhood experiences has been distributed to adults throughout California and, more recently, in Philadelphia. The questionnaire consists of 10 questions—when tabulated, it gives someone an ACES score. An ACES score, which is a representative metric of childhood trauma, acts as an uncanny predictor of adult physical and mental health suffering.

The manifestations of early childhood trauma range from increased rates of diabetes and cancer to inarguably disturbing rates of depression, anxiety, and PTSD. High ACES scores also seem to occur in tandem with childhood poverty. Childhood poverty typically leaves children living in environments that are infiltrated with toxic and chronic stress. This stress is the byproduct of families living in abject scarcity, often hunger, significant violence, and with constant feelings of heightened fear and terror.

Although we are aware of the immutable vulnerability of the developing mind from the ages of 0-3, this vulnerability seems to extend to the age of 6. The more stress there is in the childhood environment, both inside the home and outside of it, the more the developing mind is compromised. Children living in chronic, chaotic, and toxic stress operate mainly out of the base of their brains, where the hypothalamic-pituitary-adrenal axis (HPA axis) exists. Operating and surviving from this neurobiological realm prevents the development of executive functioning, which is born out of the frontal lobe. Development literally cannot occur because of the child's effort to regulate the stimuli of a stressful environment. Beyond the age of 6, the possibility of developing successful frontal lobe functionality becomes increasingly difficult.

Of course, as social workers, we know all this. Perhaps we were taught it, or perhaps we bear witness to it daily. Either way, we know and we know it deeply. Maybe we don't literally know that only 14% of Philadelphia fourth graders are at the proper reading level, but we do know that our children are drowning in their own cortisol and adrenaline. Maybe we don't literally know that more than 62 people were shot over Memorial Day Weekend (2016) in Chicago, but we know that our children are often too scared to risk their own vulnerability to the possibility of attachment. We know that our clients are suffering. And make no mistake about it, the people suffering the most are our clients.

When allowing ourselves to think clearly about the nearly depraved state of inequality that currently exists in our country, it is hard to remain engaged and determined. Of course, policy changes are essential, and we won't heal without them. However, the most basic social work interventions are the precise leverage in the war that is being waged against poor people. How do we develop frontal lobe functionality? How do we reduce cortisol levels? How do we keep people from acting out of impulse rather than deliberation and intent? The answer to all of these questions, all of the time, is through relationship.

> **For every way our society is structured to annihilate the evolution of authentic equality, the clinical social work relationship offers an antidote.**

The cornerstone of clinical social work practice is the relationship, again and again, over and over. The relationship, meaning the presence of a steady attachment figure that offers empathy, curiosity, and warmth, shifts neurobiology. It doesn't just shift it. It also lends to the development of more complex cognitive and affective functionality. In the presence of a steady, mirroring relationship, the brain calms down in profound ways. This calm, almost like a fertilizer, lends to the development of meta-cognition and reflective functioning. Reflective functioning, the opposite of the fight or flight response, requires the use of the frontal lobe and allows for decision making.

Aside from theoretical orientation, specific interventions, treatment planning, or goal making, the relationship itself is what is curative—and curative in profound ways. For every way our society is structured to annihilate the evolution of authentic equality, the clinical social work relationship offers an antidote. Is it a sufficient antidote? Certainly not. But does it penetrate growing minds, creating the possibility for secure attachment experiences? Yes, absolutely.

By showing up, asking good questions, maintaining eye contact, meeting consistently, and seeing people holistically, we begin to help people experience themselves as cohesive wholes. When feeling overwhelmed by the pain around us, it is utterly essential to remember that it is exactly what we have been trained to do that can turn tides. The tide changes might not be immediately obvious or fully satisfying, but all corrective attachment experiences are cumulative. We are piecing together an extended release treatment that will emit its effects, in the minds of our clients over time, often unbeknownst to our searching eyes.

Strawberry

I hate taking pictures with cars in them, unless there is some purposeful role that the cars can play. This is typically quite challenging, because cars are everywhere. In this picture, the sheer beauty of the strawberry makes the cars necessarily embarrassing. They don't hold a candle to the strawberry. The strawberry, perfectly red and seeded, was lying in the parking lot at Target. Amidst consumerism, the strawberry begged for my attention. It was trying to remind me that there was nothing I needed beyond what the earth had to offer.

15. Deciphering Trauma

As social workers, we are constantly faced with the difficult work of managing the resulting symptoms of traumatic events. Part of this management requires us to delineate between the presentation of trauma and other mental health struggles, such as depression, anxiety, or grief. Trauma, while appearing to have many overlapping symptoms with other conditions, truly operates in its own way, residing in a specific place in both the brain and the body. Many who are negotiating the stress and torment over what happened in Orlando are certainly feeling grief stricken and startled. This does not mean that everyone is traumatized because of it. However, for massacres and other attachment assaults, trauma is a common outcome, made better only by the proper and precise identification and subsequently well attuned treatment of it.

Trauma is not anxiety.

Anxiety is often associated with trauma; however, it is not the same as trauma itself. Anxiety is often experienced as a dysregulation in the flow of both adrenaline (the chemical that courses through us when in a flight mode) and cortisol (the chemical that runs through us when we are in a fight mode). Similar to depression, anxiety is highly based in the body and mind. The body feels nearly electrified, while the mind runs through an unmanageable volume of thoughts, which are typically described as worries. Sometimes the thoughts are obsessive and feel nearly impossible to get a hold of. When relief comes through experiencing a rational or soothing thought, another set of frightening thoughts often follows. Finding calm in a sea of anxiety is extremely difficult, given the heavy role that our limbic system plays in sustaining anxious states. Furthermore, when the body can no longer sustain anxious states, depression typically follows.

Trauma is not depression.

Although many people experience depression as a result of trauma, trauma and depression are two distinct psychological phenomena. The central signs of depression are a decrease in motivation, loss of interest in familiar and enjoyable activities, and an overwhelming feeling of hopelessness. Individuals who are depressed try to seek ways to self soothe, but they have difficulty identifying ways to do so. Many who feel depressed describe feeling as if their minds are blank and that it is hard to give words to their thought processes. Depression can almost feel flu-like, slowing down the overall body and mind. It is an extremely painful way to feel, because the road to relief feels paved with tasks that feel impossible, like exercise, social engagement, and talking openly.

Trauma is not grief.

Grief, the complex set of emotions that follow a loss, is typically experienced in five stages. Although these stages are not always linear, there is a somewhat predictable format to the grief experience. These stages are denial, anger, bargaining, depression, and acceptance. There is no set timeline for these stages, and some parts of the grieving process last much longer than others. Grief, most commonly characterized by sadness, is a completely natural part of attachment and loss. There is nothing wrong with grief. In fact, grief needs to be experienced for us to metabolize loss.

What is trauma?

The way trauma is distinct from psychological processes mentioned above is that it is an assault on the body and the psyche. First, someone can experience a trauma and not become traumatized. The single biggest predictor of whether or not someone becomes traumatized by a trauma (a car accident, a murder, a robbery, an illness) is the presence of a secure attachment. Secure attachment, at any

> **The single biggest predictor of whether or not someone becomes traumatized by a trauma is the presence of a secure attachment.**

point in someone's life, can act as a protective factor against someone becoming traumatized. Furthermore, becoming traumatized is not the same thing as developing PTSD or complex PTSD.

There are different levels at which trauma resides in us, the most superficial being called "traumatized" and the most penetrating level being characterized as complex trauma. PTSD lies somewhere in between. When someone is traumatized, this often means that the person is in a hypervigilant state, marked by the presence of intrusive thoughts. But there is an awareness of the distinction between their sense of self and what happened to them. PTSD, more deep seated, does start to seep into one's sense of self and causes tremendous levels of dysregulation, irritability, reoccurring images of the stressor, and leaves someone generally operating from a place of fight or flight. Most disturbing to one's sense of self is complex PT3D. Complex PTSD suggests the presence of a prolonged trauma, extensive exposure to a stressful environment, extremely unpredictable attachment experiences, and a near inability to distinguish between one's sense of self versus the trauma itself.

It is essential for us, clinically, to properly assess traumatization. This is because, without proper treatment, trauma begets trauma. The more unresolved that trauma is, the more malignantly it has an impact on our overall environments. Furthermore, psychological trauma results in a loss of faith in the order of the world, in the possibility of meaning making, and creates an unending inability to find safety within one's own mind or relationships. Our lives feel completely unmanageable to us when we cannot find meaning, and this leaves us fleeing our own minds at almost any expense, including dissociation, rage, and possible psychosis.

Treating trauma

The most valuable element of any treatment of trauma is that the trauma is *named* and that the client is *believed*. Taken from the shaken and traumatized client is a sense of their own truth, own believability, own sense of knowing. In our work, we must diligently attend to the work of helping our clients re-know their own truth, but reflecting back to them what we are hearing. We must also help to educate them on the fact that self-doubt is a hallmark of trauma, not evidence of the absence of it. Another task in our work with traumatized clients is to encourage, though in a well-paced manner, the telling and retelling of their stories. For some, this might be too difficult to handle, and that is okay. Others can tell small parts of their stories. For others, talking about issues or stories that resemble their own helps, too. The bottom line is to help clients to see the trauma as separate from their own sense of self.

Another central piece of our work with trauma is to remain as predictable and transparent in our work as possible. While we cannot necessarily create perfectly secure attachments, the very nature of our ability to contain the rhythm of the clinical process can help someone to feel as if the world is less chaotic and fearful.

Trauma work requires engagement with intense affect. We cannot keep our emotions out of our work with trauma. Concurrently, we ought to tenderly offer a persistent and open invitation to the emotions of our clients—the good, bad, and ugly.

While trauma work is clearly complicated and deserves complex attention and study, there are basic tenets that can create real and lasting change. Recognizing the way that trauma lives in the body and mind, the way it is distinct from other mental health issues (although there is tremendous overlap), and honoring the way it overwhelms *or* severs one's mind from intolerable realities can start to pave a path toward relief.

16. Emotional Acres of Land/ Black Lives Matter

I have long been struck by the notion of helping our clients to claim "an emotional acre of land." The concept suggests that well-being is linked to our ability to have a private psychological space to think, feel, and be. The theory behind the acre is that the more intruded upon our psychic lives are, the less likely we are to feel safe, held, and ultimately, productive.

Then, two Black men lost their lives to police in one week, and I noticed that my own emotional acre of land quickly vanished, in-truded upon by startling images of violent injustice and horrifying loss. And the fact is, that as a White woman, I am lucky to ever have access to this emotional acre, given how many people in our country are deprived of not only having rich psychological lives, but of having life at all.

I could offer shocking statistics about racial inequity in this coun-try, but the fact is that I probably don't have access to anything that you haven't already read. I am sure you might have read that a man named Philando Castile was killed by police or that Alton Sterling was a homeless man, trying to raise his family in a shelter by selling CDs on the street. Or perhaps you read that a White man newly re-leased from prison is as likely to be hired as a Black man who is newly graduated from college. I am sure you saw that Black men represent 9% of Americans but more than 40% of the unarmed people killed by American police. Or that an unarmed Black man is 700% more likely to be killed by police than an unarmed White man.

But what do the numbers do? Not much. What do the videos, tweets, and Facebook posts do? Well, they typically fade. How can we stay awake? How can we allow our clients—the oppressed, marginal-ized, and suffering—to acquire both the literal and metaphoric acres of land that they are past due?

For me, I return to the NASW *Code of Ethics,* our own personal constitution. The preamble states:

The primary mission of the social work profession is to enhance human well-being and help meet the basic human needs of all people, with attention to the needs and empowerment of people who are vulnerable, oppressed, and living in poverty. A historic and defining feature of social work is the profession's focus on individual well-being in a social context and the well-being of society. Fundamental to social work is attention to the environmental forces that create, contribute to, and address problems in living.

NASW, 2008

What this means, of course, to do our jobs honorably, is that we must consistently and vigilantly unlearn racism, and give voice to those whose voices are hoarse, strained, disappeared. But that is broad and hard to apply. The real question is: *How do we maintain an eye on the byproducts of violent oppression while practicing clinical social work?* And in answering this question, we ought to attend to staying awakened in a sustained and focused way, to ultimately shift the amount of spaces that our clients can rest their minds within.

When working with people of color, as a White clinician (and please note the remainder of this is directed to White clinicians), the more consistently we invite feelings of fear and lack of safety into our work, the more permission we give to address these issues. We have to walk a fine line between both knowing about the depths of oppression, and at the same time realizing that we can never fully understand. While there are ways in which some oppressions overlap, the unique experience of feeling unsafe in the hands of law enforcement has to be recognized for its idiosyncratic psychological ramifications.

To be a part of any agency at all suggests that we are part of an overall societal structure that serves to perpetuate oppression and racial disparity. Those settings include hospitals, schools, social service organizations, adoption agencies. The list goes on. The fact is that to be a part of almost any organized structure in American society is to be part of a system of racialized functioning. It is in the interest of our *Code of Ethics* to carefully study the ways in which this is occurring in all of our work settings and to subsequently make this transparent to our clients. For example, if you are part of a division of human services making a visit to a home of a Black family, it is worth saying, "I want to know how it feels to have me visiting you," "What is your perception of this organization," and "I am sorry for the ways that this organization may have disrupted your community or family in the past."

We often think that by not addressing race, we are somehow all at peace. Although we would not consciously claim this, it is implied by our silence. The fact is that in any heterogenic racial pairing, race is a relational factor. The more we commit to being transparent about this, the more productive and deep our clinical relationships can become.

It is also our work to surrender any defensiveness we feel about our own racism. The fact is that to live in America is to be racist. Perhaps this is true in other countries, as well, but I cannot speak as clearly to that. Despite how impassioned we are about equality, this does not shift our very real unconscious biases. And more importantly, it does not shift how powerfully these unconscious biases are activated when we have depleted internal resources. We are depleted of internal resources when we are scared, overworked, undersupervised. These very real social work issues diminish us to our base instincts, leaving us functioning in a far less empathic and culturally relativistic manner.

In this surrendering, it is also our clinical duty to consider the real psychological ramifications of living in a society that is skewed away from justice for your family and community. The tension between many police officers and Black communities leaves members of those communities in a heightened and vigilant state, akin to what PTSD looks and feels like. To not be able to comfortably and confidently call the police if you are being robbed, if you have a loved one who has fallen, or if you cut yourself with the kitchen knife, is to live in a world that is inherently unsafe. The central tenet underlying the possibility for human growth and development is a feeling of safety. In other words, huge portions of our country are deprived of the psychological resources to comfortably grow into our world. Additionally, seeing that there has been no justice taken while Black lives have inexplicably and viciously ended furthers how much our world is impairing the possibility of providing emotional acres of land within which to reside and grow.

Clinically, our work comes down to the provision of an emotional acre of land for each of our clients. For our clients of color, this requires a more generous invitation into the room. It requires an intentional invitation that honors the complexity of the state of our world, never denying our part in it. It requires an invitation that recognizes the racist past and present of our country. It requires an invitation that realizes that it might take some extra time to settle in and that our hurried work will not make this settling possible. And it requires an invitation that recognizes that rage and grief, right now, are probably the healthiest emotions anyone can feel in the face of more ordinary lives lost to extraordinary abuses of power and authority.

17. On Childhood Sexual Abuse

Although all abuse leaves the child psyche in tatters, there is perhaps no other form of abuse as devastating to the developing mind and body as sexual abuse. There are several complex reasons for this fact that are worth revisiting. But most potently, the misunderstanding of what constitutes sexual abuse might be part of what makes it so disruptive. We often think of sexual abuse as being linked to intent, when in fact there is rarely conscious intent at work when someone is being sexually abused. Instead, sexual abuse is typically the byproduct of unconscious impulses in the abuser that leave the recipient feeling overstimulated and dysregulated.

Let's start with the traditional definition of sexual abuse. Colloquially speaking, sexual abuse is considered to be molestation or undesired sexual behavior forced upon one person by another. Unfortunately, this definition leaves out a vast number of experiences of sexual exploitation and abuse. The definition relies on touch as a marker of abuse. It also relies upon the idea that the abuse is undesired, which is just too much of an oversimplification of the reality of how sexual abuse feels.

In 1932, Sandor Ferenczi, a psychoanalyst, gave a speech to a group of fellow clinicians. In this speech, he argued that there was a psychological phenomenon at play, on a societal level. He called this phenomenon "The Confusion of Tongues." In his presentation, he argued that children are not most frequently sexually abused by penetration or molestation, but instead by overstimulation. He argued that children were sexually seduced by adults who did not know how to better regulate their own sexual impulses and desires. For children, whose sexualities ought to be developing in the closed system of their own psyches, having intrusive involvement by caregivers becomes psychologically difficult to metabolize.

This seduction is not overt and can barely be named by the abuser or the child being abused. For example, a child might be overstimulated by seeing parents watch pornography. Or, children might not know how to manage seeing their parents having sex. Perhaps a child has trouble making sense of overhearing two teachers talking explicitly about the sex that they had last night. Or, perhaps a child has watched a caregiver masturbate in front of the child. None of these examples include a child being touched. None of these examples include a child's clear capacity to know that they don't want these things to happen. And none of these examples include a clear level of intent.

Ferenczi was shunned by the psychoanalytic community following his argument for parents' capacity to seduce their children. Although I don't know the exact nuances of his ostracization, I do think that it is important to begin to think more about the nuances of sexual abuse or sexual impropriety. This is important because many children are struggling with sequelae of sexual abuse but feel as if there is no clear antecedent to this symptomology. They become confused about their own burgeoning sexuality, often feeling tremendous shame, hypersexuality, or a terror about sex in general. They also feel that there is something deeply wrong with them, confused about why they feel as curious and overstimulated around sexual issues as they do.

Recognizing the broader spectrum under which sexual abuse can occur helps us to more properly help our clients. Furthermore, it can take the pressure off both the clinician and the client to find single incidents of sexual abuse. Instead, the focus can shift to developmentally misattuned environments that leave children reeling, in search of how to make sense of the material in their own minds.

Upon recognizing this broader spectrum, it is essential to recognize the idiosyncratic nature of how sexual abuse preys upon the mind. First, sexual abuse tends to rob children of their relationship with truth. Feeling unclear about what they are perceiving and feeling in their own environments, children's minds start to re-narrate what they are witnessing in favor of a more tolerable script. This flipped script leaves children unclear about whether they can safely trust their perceptions. Second, sexual abuse also leaves children with a sense that they themselves are perpetrators. Because the body is inherently aroused by sexual seduction, material, or behavior, children feel that their own bodies wished for this and, therefore, it is somehow their fault. Further, because bodily sensations are experienced as a source of shame, because of their involuntary responsiveness to sexual stimuli, the child tries to disconnect from all the information that the body provides. This can lead to problems with bladder infections, incontinence, or just plain confusion about what the body desires.

Our work with sexually abused children almost always leaves us struggling in our own haze of confusion and doubt. The tendency for children to pathologically doubt themselves seeps into our treatment, often leaving us doubtful about how we are proceeding, if we are having any impact at all, or if our children are even telling the truth. Perhaps this is why treatment of sexually abused children has become almost compulsively manualized—aiming us to avoid the inevitable confusion brought on by this work.

To successfully treat children who have been sexually abused, several paradigm shifts are required. This means, primarily, that we need to reconceptualize the possible scope of sexual abuse. This reconceptualization can free us from seeking someone to blame, instead offering a refocusing on the suffering client in front of us. Also, instead of fighting the powerful discomfort that comes with working with sexually abused children, we can occupy and tolerate the doubt. The doubt gives us access to our clients' own psychological experiences, as well as offering them a respite from the demanding doubts in their own minds. We also need to recognize the dual impact that sexual abuse has on the mind and the body. While sexual abuse often serves to sever the mind/body connection by creating bodily experiences that are intolerable for the mind to process, our work can re-link these two ultimately inseparable entities by inviting both into the room.

PART 3
Diagnosis and Beyond

Messaging

When looking for pictures to take, I am often struck by the messages that are made available to me. In the middle of a long walk—doubting my ability to produce any worthwhile photography, doubting the quality of my camera, of my vision—I found the words "tired of being humble." The messages around us abound, if we pay enough attention.

18. The Chicken, the Egg, and the DSM

There is something inherently redundant about having a conversation about diagnosis. As social workers, we agree that there is a lot about diagnosis that is incredibly problematic. We also find ways to work in systems that make use of, if not over rely upon, diagnosis. We try and exert astounding amounts of energy thinking both diagnostically and holistically, often occupying multiple states of conceptualization at the same time. We create treatment plans in accordance with diagnosis and create goals with it in mind, too. We do a crazy dance to keep the client from knowing what we are thinking diagnostically, while attending to diagnosis in supervision and in team meetings. We bill according to it, we think about medication in light of it, and we often create interventions with it in mind. All the while, we are feeling quite uncomfortable with the fact of diagnosis and questioning its destructive power.

I have a client who was diagnosed with ODD when he was 7 years old. He kicked a kid (really hard) and was discharged from his school. When he was 9 years old, he was diagnosed with Asperger's syndrome, before it was understood as a place on the autism spectrum. He didn't have a lot of friends and often wandered around the school playground alone. When he was 16, he was diagnosed with bipolar disorder and was put on several anti-psychotic medications, including lithium, Abilify®, and Risperdal®. Perhaps this trajectory of diagnoses sounds extreme. I can assure you, it is not. In fact, it is startlingly common.

Today, he is not on any medication and feels terrified to see a psychiatrist, though he could probably benefit from an antidepressant for his very low moods. When he talks about being diagnosed with Asperger's, he talks about how this infiltrated his sense of self. He was told that he was poor at socializing, that his eye contact was sub-par, that he fixated on one or two subjects, and that he needed to diversify his interests to ever make friends. He spent years of his life socially isolated, in his bedroom, playing video games. He imagined that he could never develop socialization skills because he simply didn't have them. Born wrong.

Chicken. Egg. Egg. Chicken.

Let's hypothesize that his original ODD diagnosis scared him about his own power and aggression so much that he decided that the best way to self-regulate, at a young age, was to turn totally inward. In turning inward, he shut down his desire for connection and for attachment. The desire was so overwhelming that he stopped even looking people in the eye and took comfort, only, in the musings of his own mind. As a byproduct of this comfort, he started to find a few powerful interests. He fell in love with the possibility of space travel and Vatican history. The topics are somewhat obscure, sure. But they also guaranteed him the self-regulation he was looking for. If he had become obsessed with video games, he would have wanted to talk to other kids about it. But he had come to believe that he was terrifying to other kids and that he might hurt them. So, it was best to have odd interests that didn't interest others.

Entering early adolescence, the loneliness became unbearable. He found that he was devastated by the loneliness, poorly versed in how to connect with others. So, he would drink and use excessive amounts of drugs to drown out his inhibitions. When high on drugs, typically cocaine, he would lose complete control of his impulses. He once walked down a busy set of train tracks just to see what would happen. Another time, he spent more than $1,000 of his very low-income parents' money to throw a huge party. The bipolar diagnosis, of course, made sense.

We know that diagnosis is reductive and doesn't honor the complex idiosyncrasy of the human mind. We also know, on some level, that it can be used as a form of social control. For example, African American men are diagnosed with schizophrenia at levels that are four to five times more than other groups. Following the diagnosis, of course, comes the intense medication. That means that there are portions of our population that are being medicated for diagnoses that are unevenly distributed among ethnic and socioeconomic groups. That is just plain dangerous.

But we also know that we can't surrender it completely. For a social worker in a school, the only way to even get a student an IEP (individualized education plan) is through the use of a mental health diagnosis. For many who are suffering the negative psychological impact of ravaging poverty, the only way to receive Social Security disability benefits is through use of a diagnosis. For veterans, the only way to become service connected for therapy is through diagnosis. So, we just do it. We do what we have to do and we fill out the DSM code and move on.

I think I am wondering if we can ever move on, though.

I am not suggesting that we give up on diagnosis. That, too, would be as reductive as diagnosis can be. It would also negate the number of people who feel unbelievably relieved by diagnosis because it helps them to better understand themselves. I do think, though, that we need to seriously question a few things. First, can we ever diagnose someone and return to thinking of them in a way that is free of that diagnosis? Second, is there a way we can use diagnosis that keeps us from being completely complicit in a system that oppresses our clients? Third, is there a way to use diagnosis that will allow us to remain steadfastly aware of the actual underlying debilitating impact of racism, sexism, poverty, and discrimination?

> **Can we ever diagnose someone and return to thinking of them in a way that is free of that diagnosis?**

I am not sure of the answers to these questions. I know that when I am thinking diagnostically, I am fleeing the intimacy of a clinical encounter. For example, when my client above doesn't make eye contact with me, I find myself wondering if he *really* does have Asperger's syndrome. In that curiosity, I am removed from how the material we are talking about is painful and making eye contact only makes him feel more unbearably vulnerable. When I have a client who can't keep a job, I start to wonder about whether or not that client has a borderline level of instability. Instead of working on the grief, rejection, and destabilization that come from not sustaining employment, I start to intellectualize.

I picture my big purple book, which used to be gray, and flip a list of bullet points in my mind.

19. In the Realm of Personality Disorders

Upon preparing to release the *DSM 5*, there was a large push to shift the way that we think about personality disorders. Rather than understanding the personality disorders as discrete, the hope was that we could move toward thinking about personality disorders as more complex and dimensional. Essentially, the argument was for more dimensional thinking regarding personality disorders. It seems that instead of personality disorders occurring in discrete categories, there is a tremendous amount of overlap between disordered characteristics.

Without taking too much of a stance on this either way, I want to share some thoughts on how deep work with personality disorders can feel. I also want to address the ways in which one can identify the presence of a personality disorder.

As social workers, we are loathe to identify personality disorders, because they have long been deemed as untreatable. This is certainly not my experience. However, the identification of the presence of a personality disorder does seem paramount to the possibility of its subsequent amelioration.

First, let me be clear. I am largely referring to a few different personality disorders: *narcissistic, borderline, histrionic,* and *obsessive-compulsive personality disorder.* These personality disorders can best be diagnosed by the studying of one's own countertransferential response to a client. There is a distinct experience in the countertransference that arises in working with personality disorders.

This experience is the byproduct of the developmental arrests in the psychological development of the client. Because personality disorders are largely born out of a failure to mature, individuals who struggle with them don't typically have a fully formed sense of self. The fragmented self is held together by a body, but not the mind. Instead, the mind has several distinct entities that the self is not fully comfortable with. The entities that bring the most discomfort, like self-hatred or misanthropy, end up entering the relational environment and often get lodged in the mind of the clinician. The entities that bring the most comfort, like grandiosity or self-righteousness, become inflated in the presence of others, while the others work to metabolize the more difficult aspects of the self.

From a countertransferential perspective, this means that we can become quite encumbered by the psyches of our clients. During sessions, we might feel confused and disoriented. We often experience tremendous self-doubt about our word choices and interventions. In the presence of a person with a personality disorder, we often feel most swayed to bend our boundaries and to shift the frame. We leave sessions feeling hung over. This hangover can lead to the presence of our clients in our unconscious minds, often entering our dreams and distant thoughts.

The most difficult part of our work with personality disorders is that we are often left with profound feelings of self-hatred. These feelings of self-hatred are frequently defended against, by individual therapists and agencies, by dismissing more personality disordered clients as manipulative, incurable, and taxing.

So, what is going on when we are working with a client with a personality disorder? Simply put, people with personality disorders feel lost within their own minds. Their minds don't seem to make coherent sense and are often intruded upon by unwelcome thoughts and feelings. To try and regulate these thoughts and feelings, the fragments get launched into the environment and breed in the minds of others. This is why you might go into a session feeling okay and leave a session feeling absolutely horrible, but you are unclear about why or what even happened. A psychological transaction occurred that allowed for the self-regulation of the client, at the expense of square footage in the mind of the clinician.

What makes all of this more difficult, unfortunately, is what differentiates someone with what was previously (prior to the advent of the DSM-5) conceived as an Axis 1 disorder from someone with an Axis II disorder. These feelings and thoughts feel completely true and real at all times. For example, someone with major depressive disorder (an Axis I diagnosis) might have extreme disgust at their lack of motivation. However, the lack of motivation bothers them and it feels like something that might not be a fixed aspect of who they are. When someone with an Axis II disorder experiences a lack of motivation, this becomes the entire lens through which they understand themselves.

Furthermore, while environmental circumstances increase the intensity and furor of Axis I symptoms, Axis II symptoms often persist regardless of environmental relief. In fact, sometimes more supportive environments can make symptoms worse, because one's sense of self is so distinct from how the supportive environment feels. This means that as we increase our offerings of empathy, our clients can become enraged with us and work to destroy our relationships with them.

Very simply put, each personality disorder bleeds into the next. However, there are some tell-tale signs of each specific realm.

Here are some great countertransference clues.

When working with **obsessive compulsive personality disorder,** you will likely feel:

- ashamed about your relationship with authority
- as if you are not properly following the rules of treatment
- that you are on the receiving end of significant, yet elusive, passive aggression.

This is because obsessive compulsive personality disorder is defined by a collapsed sense of right and wrong and is supplanted by an overactive superego that leads the client to operate in an almost constant sense of shame. This shame is only regulated by extreme attention to rules and boundaries and the excessive regulation of those around them.

When working with **borderline personality disorder,** you will likely feel:

- split from your colleagues, haunted by a sense of distrust of the environment that you are working in
- a sense of relational unpredictability, never sure if you are saving or destroying your client
- significant suspicion about most of the people in the life of your client
- that you are never doing enough.

This is because borderline personality disorder is characterized by an unwieldy sense of self. The client shifts between extreme feelings of confidence and loathing. Clients feel vacillating distrust in themselves or in their relationships, always struggling to hold ambiguity and complexity.

When working with **narcissistic personality disorder,** you will likely feel:

- you are deeply charmed by your clients and wonder why they aren't more successful in their lives
- you are somehow being used in the service of your client and that your client has very little interest in who you are

- you could be interchangeable with another therapist and it might not change a thing.

This is because narcissistic personality disorder is characterized by an unending crisis in the sustaining of an even level of self-esteem. Most relational decisions are made in the service of regulating one's idea about one's own goodness.

When working with **histrionic personality disorder,** you will likely feel:

- highly moved toward action, emboldened by a wish to "fix" everything that a client introduces
- surprised by how much has gone wrong in your client's life
- unable to discern the level of import of the data presented by your client.

This is because histrionic personality disorder is most characterized by an inability to regulate the level of importance of internal and external stimuli. Every feeling and life event is experienced with the same level of intensity and fear. The client will work diligently to alert you to these crises, hoping to feel less alone in the management of these experiences.

Uniting these disorders are several themes:

- an inability to entertain the subjective experience of another
- the use of others to regulate one's own experience of oneself
- extreme disregulation of affective states
- paranoid thoughts and delusions
- distrust in systems around them
- the ability to create chaos, while making it very difficult to identify the source of this chaos.

The central treatment tenets for working with personality disorders are:

- the careful studying of countertransferential data
- predictable and constant boundary setting
- a guarding against the settling in fragments from the client's mind into your own
- extensive use of supervision
- a steady belief in the possibility of treatment serving to help mature the mind of the client, allowing for a solid experience of one's self.

Showcasing

Sometimes it seems like nature arranges itself to brag. Getting into my car on the way to work, I looked down and saw this perfect arrangement. It seems as if the aging leaves agreed to let the red leaf have its day in the sun. I like to think about the leaves discussing this among themselves.

20. On Narcissism and Its Discontents

One of the most disorienting and destabilizing dynamics that we face in relationships is to be intimately involved with someone who has narcissistic tendencies. While being engaged with narcissistic personality disorder renders powerful difficulties, handling any narcissistic characteristics is tricky business.

First, let's start with the origins of the story of Narcissus, a character in Greek mythology. Narcissus was proud of his capacity to hate those who loved him most. In response to this, Nemesis took Narcissus to a pool of water, where he fell in love with his own image. He fell so in love with his image, in fact, that he never left the reflection—dying in the act of staring at himself. Superficially, it would seem that he was enamored with his own gaze, but the more underlying truth of the story is that he lost touch with who he was when he looked away. He was not able to maintain a steady sense of self without a clear reflection staring back at him.

In the story of Narcissus, we are introduced to a familiar character. This is a character we all have in our lives, whether as a client, a supervisor, or a parent. We have archetypes of Narcissus all around us, because narcissists are simply people whose developmental needs were not met. For people to develop a solid and steady sense of self, they require environmental mirroring. Basically, what that means is that for people to figure out who they are, they need to see reflections of themselves in others. For example, if a child falls and gets hurt, that child needs to hear, "Oh, that looks like it really hurts." If the pain is ignored, it is nearly impossible to modulate and make sense of it. Or, let's think of someone who has an internal sense of same sex attraction but sees no one who is gay around them. It becomes very troubling to develop an understanding of one's own feelings without data around oneself to help support what is happening inside.

Not everyone who has not been properly mirrored becomes a narcissist. But it does help to understand that most narcissists have had a developmental disruption that compromised their developing sense of self. And their ability to relate becomes terrifically compromised.

Because no one has a pool like Narcissus did, offering an impeccable reflection, other resources are sought out to provide this reflection. These other resources are invariably people. Individuals with narcissistic tendencies rely on others to inform their understanding of who they are. Rather than forming three-dimensional relationships, people who are narcissistic tend to use others for reflective purposes. This means that you are used most powerfully when you provide a satisfying and soothing reflection. You become most useless when the reflection that you provide disappoints the narcissistic person's perception of who they are.

Individuals with narcissistic tendencies, basically, function in a constant crisis around their self-esteem. Rather than being driven by attachment, which many of us are, more narcissistic folks are driven by the wish to experience a stable sense of worth. And their sense of worth, because it is so underdeveloped, is something that they are always searching to regulate. Like those who permanently have their finger on a thermostat, narcissists use others to turn the temperature up or down, depending on how they are feeling at any given moment.

The impact that this has on the person who is working with or interacting with a narcissist is what truly needs to be honored and recognized. This is because some of our most painful relational interactions occur when interfacing with someone who is narcissistic. There are some primary ways in which this pain is inflicted.

Projective identification

One of the most predictable ways in which someone narcissistic self-regulates is through the defense of *projective identification*. Projective identification occurs when narcissistic people siphon off a part of themselves that they hate, which disrupts their sense of self, and lodges this part of them into your own mind or psyche. For example, let's say you are seeing a doctor who struggles with narcissism. The doctor thinks, "I am unsure of what I am doing," and can't tolerate that feeling. The doctor will self-regulate by disavowing this sensation and somehow send it into the psyche of the patient. The patient then becomes overwhelmed by feelings of incompetence, starts to stutter, and doesn't know what to say next. The doctor leaves the appointment feeling oddly confident, and the patient feels like a fool. It is almost impossible to say when the moment of transaction occurs, but it does. And it occurs most easily when there is a pre-existing vulnerability to whatever feeling the narcissist wants to shed. This is particularly true in an established power dynamic, like the doctor and patient in this example.

Gaslighting

The term *gaslighting* captures an abusive phenomenon that typically occurs between narcissistic individuals and the people who are most attached to them. It is a tactic by which victims are left to question their own perceptions of reality, when the scripts get flipped and the events that have occurred are re-authored by the narcissistic member of the dyad. Typically, what occurs is that an upsetting transgression takes place. For example, someone is walked in on when naked or someone's journal is read. When the victims of these intrusions voice discomfort about what has occurred, they are somehow confused that the occurrence is their fault. Narcissists will argue that the door was unlocked and it seemed like an invitation or that the journal had to be read because of how insecure they were feeling in the relationship.

It is nearly impossible for people with narcissistic tendencies to take responsibility for their actions. It seems to invariably be the fault of the *other*. However, this does not mean that narcissistic individuals won't try to right their wrongs. It is just that this will only occur when it makes narcissists feel better about themselves and improves their self-esteem in that exact moment. Typically, apologies take the form of grand gestures, almost serving as the pool of reflection in which Narcissus first studied his own image.

Charm

Part of why those of us who have close relationships with narcissists feel so confused about our experiences is because those with narcissistic characteristics are typically well and widely liked. Our experiences of them completely confound us when we see how they are viewed in more public settings. Individuals with narcissistic tendencies know how to seduce others, make others feel amazing and heard, and have inarguable charisma. Unfortunately, these characteristics only sustain themselves insofar as they help the narcissists regulate their self-esteem. In more private interactions, without a group to reflect the desired need for grandeur, the sense of self collapses and the people closest to the narcissist suffer the backlash.

So what?

Narcissism feels important to talk about at this particular moment because it is all around us. It is certainly being seen in politics and on the public stage. Further, with increased pools of water (meaning Instagram, Snapchat, Facebook), the reliance on reflection to refine one's sense of self is quite powerful right now. Also, recognizing the potholes of working with narcissists is an essential self-care strategy that will help you sustain your energy over time.

Simply put, narcissism is a byproduct of arrested development and under-recognition at critical times in the evolution of one's sense of self. It can be remedied, but it is very difficult to do. The more that an authentic version of the narcissist's internal world is understood and loved, along with their true desire for affection and affirmation, the more possible it is for them to develop beyond acting out harshly or erasing the psychological experiences of others.

By seeing that there is tenderness and vulnerability behind the vicious veil that narcissism can often wear, we can help the need for the veil to diminish. This diminishing is the direct result of being loved and seen, but it cannot occur if we hate ourselves in the service of this love.

PART 4
Our Clinical-Internal Worlds

Path

The ultimate metaphor that a picture can offer is of the unknown quantities that we are faced with on any journey. Paths with no clear endpoint feel representative of uncertainty as a fact of life. But to pause and look around the path and observe what is all around us makes that uncertainty more bearable.

21. Can We Ever Take Our Hats Off?

I often think about the many ways our psyches are constrained by the constant offering of false dichotomies. Social work is filled with them. For example, the notion that we are any different from our clients is a false dichotomy. There is also a false dichotomy between ethical and unethical. While there are certainly clinical decisions that clearly fall under each heading, many of our choices are more muddied than we would like. Perhaps most frustrating, to me, is the false dichotomy that is positioned around the supposed distinction between our professional and personal selves. We are asked, often, to keep our work at the office. We are also asked to somehow keep our clients in a very specific part of our psyche, as if thoughts and feelings actually have specific storage bins (perhaps sold at The Container Store).

I was thinking about this issue quite a bit on Halloween when something very strange happened to the families I was trick-or-treating with. A young boy was dropped off by his caregiver to go trick-or-treating on the corner of my city street in Philadelphia. He asked if he could join us. We had never met him before, but the kids I was with accepted him readily. His caretaker followed up in her car until she came to a stop sign and said that she was going to park. Several minutes later, it became clear that she had disappeared. As time passed, the boy became more and more integrated into our little group of families. The moms I was with started to get worried about what was really going on. Everyone was talking about what to do. I easily launched into an effortless assessment with him based on the rapport that we had built over the last block. I asked him about his phone number, his address, where his mom might be. He told me that he needed a GPS on me so that he couldn't lose me, evidencing some complicated attachment tendencies on his part.

Honestly, the situation was heartbreaking. He told me that he was 5. He didn't know his phone number. He hadn't had dinner. He told me that his mom needed to go to Target because there was a sale on paper towels, and that is probably where she was.

It became clear that there was nothing benign about this situation, and all the parents agreed. However, I was clearly in charge of the assessment and the decision making. I know many of you feel this way a lot. You are a social worker "on the job," and you are a social worker "off the job." The reason why is because, in many ways, there is no discernible difference. Where there is suffering, we are on. For starters, we are mandated reporters. So the other parents that I was with actually didn't have the same level of responsibility that I did. Further, though, we have a skill set that is useful and versatile across many settings, whether we find ourselves on a street corner or in a treatment room.

So, rest doesn't come easily.

A few days later, I found out that a dearly beloved family friend had died suddenly. This was someone I have been attached to for my entire life. When I got the news, I was completely stunned. My social worker self was nowhere in sight. And I am so glad about that, because it means that I could be authentically present for the grief, sadness, and time with my family.

There is a significant contrast between these two situations, and I think that it is worth highlighting. I think it is worth highlighting because, yes, there is a distinction between our professional and personal selves. But the line doesn't fall exactly where we are told it does. I think that we, as social workers, often feel ashamed of just how social work-y we are. You hear it all the time in reductive phrases like, "Oh, you must be analyzing me right now," or "You must have a real bleeding heart to work so hard for so little," or "You really think you can save the world, don't you?" These lines suggest that we don't know when to turn it off, right? These lines suggest that we are addicted to our work somehow and that there is something wrong with us.

The fact is that there are a lot of ways that the world is unsafe and scary, and, yes, we are watching out for others all the time. But when we are called to be vulnerable, human, and raw, we are just as human as anyone else. We don't take off our hats when some arbitrary rule says that work is over at 5:00 p.m., or a session ends after 45 minutes, or discharge should occur within three days. It isn't that we can never take our social work hats off. It is that we do so selectively, carefully, and when our souls most need us to.

So, as a trick-or-treating parent, yes, I called the kid's school. And as a grieving loved one, I am taking care of myself and my family. And this is because I, like you, have the capacity to be many things, even when the division between my different selves is not as obvious and neat to others.

22. Stinging Stoicism

I have a client I have been working with for about five or six years. I have watched her make all sorts of life decisions that haven't seemed to fit her authentic desires. I watched her marry a man she was unsure about, pursue several jobs that she was not a good fit for, enable her very drug addicted mother, refuse to get a handle on her financial life. At all of these twists and turns, I barely said anything. There were times when I wanted to scream, and there were times when I wanted to whisper. But every time, I waited for her to arrive at her own truths and her own conclusions, while I sat across from her watching.

In the middle of a session, I got a sudden and horrible pain in my arm. I had no idea what it was. It was downright startling. I wanted to whisper that I was scared. I wanted to scream that I was in pain. I didn't do either. A few minutes later, we saw a bug buzzing around, making a distractingly irritating buzz. My client wondered aloud, "What is that?" I said that I had no idea. She then looked a bit closer as the bug flew by her and said, "Oh my God, that is an enormous wasp!" She grabbed my tissue box and said, "Let's kill it!" and handed me the box of tissues. I stood on my chair with my shoes on, took the tissue box, and slammed the bug into the window, murdering it, proudly. I was self conscious, but still I found my way to killing the bug. She said, sweetly, "Aw, my hero." I said, "Actually, it stung me a few minutes ago," and raised the sleeve on my shirt. It was the first time I had let myself look at the source of the pain, which was now pink and swollen. She then said, "Wow, why didn't you say anything? Actually, how didn't you say anything?"

Perhaps I was not her hero after all.

Those were the two essential questions of our treatment. Why don't I say anything? How do I manage to continuously say nothing? I want to say that the problem was co-created, that it was the byproduct of our relationship. But that answer would be both untrue and unfair. The truth is that there is a way in which I have internalized theory about how we should practice in ways that have felt both toxic and paralyzing. I get confused about my role. I know that we "shouldn't" give advice. And I know that we are ultimately gentle guides, not sages on a stage. But should this leave us tongue tied as we watch a car veering off the road? Oftentimes, it does. But no, it shouldn't.

I think we become so afraid of our own power and influence that we hold ourselves still and we hold ourselves back. We ask a lot of questions. Sometimes we offer reflections. And at our most aggressive or active, we offer interpretations. We rarely say, though, "I am scared for you," or "This doesn't sound right to ME." We seek some sort of objectivity, hoping that we can move our clients to their own realizations with techniques that will escort them there somehow. But, typically, what truly moves someone forward is the power of a relationship that both parties are uniquely and powerfully present in.

While I certainly have no affection for wasps, I am so grateful for the one that stung me. It made me realize how deadened I can be in treatment. It made me realize just how easy it is for me to stay silent, even in the face of panic and pain. The truth is that there have been many times when I have felt stung in the presence of this client. There have been many times when I have wanted to scream: "Don't do it," "Protect yourself," and "I love you and I care about you and I don't want to see you hurt." But she didn't hear the buzzing, so she didn't know.

I know that the murder of the wasp represented a deeper death between us—the death of a fantasy objectivity, the death of technique and silence. It also represented a birth—a birth of collaboration, presence, and a shared willingness to risk the pain of intimacy.

For Thanksgiving, I received a text from her. It said, "Happy Thanksgiving Danna! I feel so grateful for having you in my life. J. Enjoy the day." My first internal responses were all pre-sting-like. I worried about boundaries, about how I could "professionally" respond, about what another therapist would do. I thought for a while about not responding at all, as if I had never heard the buzz on the phone. A few hours later, I wrote, instead, "I feel grateful for having you in my life, too!" I wrote that because it is the whole, subjective truth, and anything other than that would have stung.

23. Invisible Bodies

Sometimes when I get dressed in the morning, I run through my day in my mind. I think about my 1:00, 2:00, and 3:00 clients. Then I hit my 4:00, and my plan for my outfit changes entirely. I think to myself, "I can't wear that in front of that client," or "I wore that last week and my client will remember it." What is going on with these thoughts? There are so many different variations of them, and really, they are quite overwhelming. I believe that these thoughts are the byproduct of the very complicated and paradoxical experience of having a body and being a clinician.

During my second-year placement, I had a psychotic client who seemed extremely enraged at me all the time. She would often ask me to look away from her, would complain about the fact that I was an intern, and rail against her perception of my judgment of her. During one session, she said to me, "How can I be expected to sit here and look at you when you have such an ugly double chin?" On one hand, I was devastated. On the other, I just chocked her comment up to her psychosis and dismissed the pain. I brought it up in supervision, and my supervisor suggested that my client's ability to experience rage and aggression in the safety of the clinical relationship was promising progress. Maybe that was true. But what about me? What about my body? And what about her impact on my body?

While clinical social work is clearly the meeting of two minds, it is also the meeting of two intricate bodies. And for every single body, there is a mind having a complex experience of that body's existence. No one feels completely at ease in his or her body and no one has complete mastery over how to deal with that dis-ease. However, the more we focus on creating a cure that is exacted through talking, the more dis-associated from the fact of our bodies we can become.

So, here's the thing for me. Throughout my day, I go through a million different experiences of my body. Sometimes it feels too big. Sometimes it feels just right. Sometimes I feel fidgety. Sometimes (oftentimes) I need to yawn. Sometimes I feel hungry. Sometimes I want to eat, even if I am not hungry. Sometimes I want to crack my knuckles or play obsessively with my ring on my right hand.

Sessions require a lot of sitting still, and in this stillness, I experience a tremendous amount of discomfort, preoccupation, and metaphoric itchiness. I spend a lot of time, in session, trying to get rid of these feelings by ignoring them. I try to stifle my yawn or plan to snack later. Ironically, the minute a session ends, the need for the yawn, snack, or scratch goes away.

In session, my clients talk quite a bit about their own bodies. This is great and also essential. The weird thing is that they often talk about their bodies as if the body isn't in the actual treatment room. We will talk about how sex felt, how feeling fat feels, how exhausted they are. But there is something about the reflections that often feels disembodied, somehow. They talk about having felt tired at work, fat at a dinner party, enjoying sex on a recent date. It becomes secondary to bring their bodily experiences into the room.

I know that there are a lot of interventions that now focus on this, specifically mindfulness and anything that calls on us to bring awareness to something. But, truthfully, these interventions don't dominate and don't acknowledge the complexity of the reality of there being two bodies in the room together and what that feels like.

There is a lot of fear about talking about the experience of two bodies in the room, because this can inevitably lead to feelings of transgression, overstimulation, and shame. If a client is talking about recently having had sex in a fairly provocative way, can we ever really say, "Wow, I can really feel what you are saying in my body"? Certainly not. Despite this, there has to be some way to be together, bodies included, without the levels of bodily dissociation that we tend to occupy.

I have no answers to how to do that, but I have given it a lot of thought. I am currently working hard on making sense of my bodily experiences as central clinical data. And I want to be clear that I am trying to interpret this data as co-created information about what is happening between two people, not only what is happening for my client. For example, let's say that I do start to feel fidgety in a session. I am working to become curious about what that means and to engage my mind with my body. Am I feeling fidgety because there is information coming from the client that I find to be particularly triggering? Am I feeling fidgety because there is something that is not being fully psychologically articulated and is instead being physically felt?

It can become terrifying to think about how clinical material becomes lodged in the body, but I think it is much more terrifying to work toward keeping bodies out of the room. I hate it when a client brings up something sexual and I can feel it in my body. It makes me feel so ashamed. It makes me feel as if I am doing something wrong. At the same time, isn't it so important to make sense of why my body is reacting the way it is? Isn't there a way to value the information that my body is communicating, rather than shutting down the messages contained in the sensation?

It bothered me to be told that I look like I have a double chin. From some angles, maybe I do, but not all angles. Why did that client see me from that angle? What did that mean? What did it mean that I was hurt and couldn't say something? Or that I was able to dismiss her because of her psychosis? Wasn't my refusal to respond a way of saying to her that she has no impact on another being, rendering her feeling invisible herself? My erasure of my physical experience led to the erasure of her sense of impact and reality.

One of the central goals of excellent clinical work is the integration of the mind, body, and soul. It is also the integration of affect, thought, and behavior. The more we separate these entities in ourselves and in our clients, the more we are communicating that there is some sort of danger in integration. We communicate that there is real threat and danger in becoming whole. We need to risk the exact opposite possibility, by valuing our own bodies and the information given to us by them. We need to consider that once we are whole (as clinicians and clients alike), we are more alive and, therefore, more safe and in control of our lives.

Shells

Taking a walk through the woods in Philadelphia, I stumbled upon these shells that had been perfectly stacked by another passerby. I cannot even imagine how long it took to perfectly arrange these shells. Again, this is just art of art. But it is also a meditation on the meditation of another—a gift given by astute attention to nature.

24. The Anxious Social Work Mind: Part 1

If there is anything that I have come to learn about how clinical social workers feel, it is that we are an anxious bunch. The anxiety that I hear about when teaching and supervising is largely thematic, although I know it often feels more amorphous than precise and meaningful. I also know that the anxiety can feel out of control and unstoppable. Sometimes supervision helps; sometimes it makes it worse. I also know that anxiety viciously interacts with us in a way that leaves us drained, depleting us of many of our internal resources.

There is a relationship between anxiety and depression, deeply cyclical in nature, that harms our development as clinical social workers and healers. This is something that, to thrive in the field, we need to start to make sense of.

So, why so anxious? I have a few theories.

False sense of professional self

One of the main reasons I hear that social workers feel anxious is because of a sense of being an impostor. Some call it impostor syndrome, but I would rather refer to it as a false sense of professional self. The idea of a false sense of self can be linked to both object relations theory and self psychology. It is based on the notion that we have somehow suppressed our true selves in the service of maintaining our attachment to a caregiver who could not deal with the whole of who we were or who we are. An anxious mother can't stand to hear the cries of the child; the child becomes endearingly sweet to win back the affection of the mother and to soothe/coax the mother back into the attachment.

This is very relevant. On some level, I think a parallel of this occurs in many agencies. Your supervisors, bosses, and insurance companies are seeking out a very specific kind of social worker. This is a social worker who can perform a manualized treatment, accomplish specific treatment goals within a session limit, write progress notes that suggest how these treatment goals were addressed, and increase client functionality in a measurable way. So, you find ways of trying to do this. You write "progress" notes about it. On session 11, you do the psychoeducation as prescribed. Or you don't. Either way, what your client needs and what your agency is asking for is typically misaligned. You are trying incredibly hard to stay with both polarized needs. For the most part, you feel torn. Sometimes you tell your supervisor the truth, but it isn't easy, because you feel self-conscious and worried about getting in trouble. You become the kid trying to stay connected to the mother.

Meanwhile, you are sitting with a client who has no interest in talking about their trauma. But they could spend the next 10 sessions complaining about a complicated dynamic at work or with their boyfriend or girlfriend. The whole time, you are worrying about whether you are doing what you are supposed to be doing by listening to your client and by "meeting them where they are" (which you learned in school). You know that you aren't adhering to the treatment goals. You aren't seeing any measurable symptom reduction, and you certainly aren't using the manual. You make up something in your note about how you used reflective listening to lessen the presence of intrusive thoughts, and you hope that fits.

How can you not have a false sense of professional self? The fact is that to be doing our work well, at this point in time, we are often triangulated between agency/financial/insurance company/evidence-based practice demands and the bumpy human spirit and need of our clients. There is a constant tension. You are right in the middle. This does not make you a fraud, but it does leave you a pawn in a game that you must figure out how to master without undoing your authentic professional self. When we start to feel that the problem is us, the anxiety expands. When we recognize that we are part of a complex system, very similar to the complex system that our clients are in, the anxiety lessens. We can use our nuanced understanding of our circumstances to better understand our clients. Rather than to undo our ability to work, our anxiety lessens.

Fear of feelings

Another dimension of our anxiety is our fear of feeling the whole of the affectual experience of being with clients. It has been hypothesized that there are basically four core emotional states from which all of our emotions originate. These are anger, sadness, joy, and fear. I guess you could think about the movie *Inside Out* to get a sense of what it might look like inside our minds and souls. There is some thinking that suggests that our anxiety is our effort to avoid feeling, to avoid truly inhabiting our affect states. Instead of feeling sad, we feel anxious. Instead of feeling angry, we feel anxious. This list goes on. The reason why we opt for anxiety is that something internally tells us it is safer. This sounds crazy, of course, because anxiety is so unbearable. But anxiety also keeps us on the periphery of issues and feelings that scare us—that panic us.

When we hear the stories of our clients' lives, it is almost impossible to not feel overwhelmed. I had a supervisee present a case of a child who was raped between the ages of 1 and 6 before being placed in foster care, which provided no relief because of the physical abuse that was experienced. Of course, we are pulled to flee the gravity of that. How could we feel that? There is a fear that if we let it all in, it might annihilate us. This fear operates both consciously and unconsciously. When it operates unconsciously, the feelings that we avoid often become anxiety. When we avoid it consciously, the feelings that we avoid often become shame and guilt. Either way, letting the feelings in is the way forward. Perhaps there is no room for this truth in how our days speedily move along with the constant pressure to perform, always being pressed to do more with less. That said, creating space for our internal experiences, for the pain brought to us by our clients' lives, will relieve our anxiety.

And when you are feeling anxious, I know that there is nothing more that you want than relief.

Our clinical anxiety is often driven, too, by a fear of and a desire for theory. When we think about theory, we are often comforted, because it helps us understand our clients and our work. The anxiety comes because it is often hard to literally integrate theoretical thoughts into our clinical interactions. When we are not integrating theory into our clinical interactions, we start to worry that we aren't "doing anything." We worry that we don't know enough—that we haven't read enough or learned enough in school.

Anxiety about theory

I cannot even count how many times I have heard students or supervisees say that they feel as if they aren't doing anything. Part of the basis of this feeling is that when we start to reflect on what we are doing, we can't link it to our readings or to our teachings. It is hard to describe in supervision, too. A supervisor will make a suggestion, such as, "Maybe you can give your client breathing exercises." In the next session, that won't happen, of course. This is because of the idiosyncrasy of human interaction. When we talk about theory integration, we don't literally mean that you say something from an attachment perspective or from a CBT stance. The theory is supposed to give you a sense of the spirit of your work, the overall direction and possibility. You are not "doing nothing" by not thinking of theory every time you talk. In fact, you are doing something huge, and that is being with your actual client instead of a teacher, author, or supervisor. You have also likely internalized the theory in a way that almost feels nonverbal at this point.

The other piece of this is that we don't do as much as we are directed to do. We worry that we aren't doing much, because we aren't doing much. Our work truly falls under the heading of "less is more." Essentially, our work is to help clients to say more. This often requires moving out of the way. This leads us to feel that we aren't doing anything. And that is exactly what we are supposed to be doing. It is hard to write nothing in a note. It is hard to explain it in supervision, and it doesn't exactly fit a modality or theory.

> Our work truly falls under the heading of "less is more." Essentially, our work is to help clients to say more. This often requires moving out of the way.

We often just ask for our clients to tell us more. We ask them how they are feeling, and then we ask them to tell us more again. What is that intervention? Can you name it? Probably not. Does that make you less than professional? Absolutely not. It makes your work hard to explain, nuanced, and very dynamic. Minute to minute, you don't have a plan and you shouldn't. That's as hard as a job gets. Own this. Don't let the energy suck of anxiety lead you to un-know the power of your own surrender to spontaneity and the acceptance of your clients' varied processes.

25. The Anxious Social Work Mind: Part 2

The pervasive and insidious nature of anxiety when practicing clinical work can feel both dispiriting and disconcerting. There are many manifest (or superficial) reasons for us to feel anxious as clinical social workers. Our salaries are small and our caseloads are big. The acuity of mental illness that we see is high and the number of solutions available is low. We are trying to keep people safely afloat, often working against intricate bureaucratic systems that perpetuate ugly inequity and oppression. There are also latent, less obvious reasons for our anxiety. These reasons are harder to articulate and easier to fix, paradoxically. Sometimes the sheer act of bringing awareness to these underlying fears can bring relief.

Is what I am doing actually therapeutic?

There is anxiety around simply having a conversation with a client. There is fear about the flow of the conversation. We worry about the presence of too much silence. We worry that it will feel awkward. We also worry that the conversation we have with a client is not actually different *enough* from a "regular" conversation that we would have outside of treatment. We wonder how it is different from just talking to a friend. Or, we wonder how it is different from just playing with a kid.

The fact is that it is different and isn't. Both are okay. First, our conversations with clients are made therapeutic by the presence of our intention and thoughtfulness. Our conversations are made therapeutic by our effort to make meaning of all that is said. Our conversations are made different by our basic feelings of unconditional acceptance of our clients.

There are few other times when someone can have a conversation about their criminal past, their history of abuse, their drug abuse, their eating disorder, without receiving much judgment. We do our best to listen to our clients and to help them understand themselves. Our agenda is to help them to deepen their self knowledge and gain insight into the patterns in their lives. Our conversations with our clients are probably the most supportive and open that they have in their lives.

Our conversations are also made therapeutic by the presence of our observing egos. That means that we are watching ourselves in conversation and making careful decisions. Most of the things we say, we run through a little test: *Who am I saying this for? Will this help or hurt the client? Is this well timed? Is this relevant?* You all have your own tests. The presence of these tests is a verification of our observing the conversation enough to distinguish it from "regular" conversations.

Conversely, though, sometimes our conversations don't feel that different from any other conversation. This does not mean that our work is not therapeutic. We have to build a relationship somehow. I know that we all say things that make us wonder if we are "real clinicians" or "real therapists" or "real social workers." Would a real social worker be talking about what restaurants are good or the best bus routes? I don't know, but I think so. I think that a real social worker knows how to connect, and sometimes it takes time in totally banal discourse to get us there.

Do I feel too much? Do I feel too little?

One of the biggest sources of our anxiety is that we feel too strongly about our clients. There is tremendous shame associated with our feeling that our clients matter to us. Sometimes we even wish that our clients were our family or our friends. I want to emphatically normalize this. I don't know how this experience could be avoided. I certainly don't think that it should be. Our mind is not divided into sections where we store people, though there is a lot of fantasy about this possibility. Just think about your dream life: How many times have you dreamt about some variation of your dentist, your second grade teacher, and your rabbi all being in the same room? It feels insane, but it reveals a certain truth. We are compartment-free, and the more we rail against that, the more anxious we become.

We also get anxious when we hate our clients. We have this feeling that we are supposed to like all of our clients, to maintain a constant feeling of positive regard toward them. Then one of them does something that enrages or even grosses us out. We think that we need to get rid of our hatred somehow, to really help our client. We don't need to rid ourselves of rage and hate. Furthermore, we can't. The mind and feelings simply don't work that way. You can help someone even when you hate them. This hate is usually symbolic of something important. Meaning can be made of it, somehow. The hate is also emblematic of an underlying attachment issue that we can conceptualize, rather than becoming anxious about our lack of professionalism or lack of empathy.

I can relate. I can't relate.

When we have a client whose story overlaps powerfully with our own, we almost always become concerned about our capacity to therapeutically manage the work. We fear that we will be triggered. We fear that we will be brought to a place that we can't properly function within. With our rawer internal experiences, sometimes this is true. Most times, however, it is not true. It is precisely from our place of knowing that we can practice and think. When we know the interiority of someone's experience, we can visit them there and be with them in it. We can bear better witness to the depths of their story.

While we fear our overlaps, we also fear the clinical spaces that we feel we don't know. For example, being presented with a client who has a long-term heroin addiction and chronic homelessness can feel daunting to a social worker who has never lived with addiction or socioeconomic strife. We fear that we are not the *right* clinician for them. I firmly believe that inside all of us there is a piece that can understand the affectual and subjective experience of another. While superficial differences can feel terrifically glaring, subtle human connection and commonality ought not be obscured. There is something in you that can connect with any client, if you dig deeply enough.

My clients aren't getting better. My clients are getting worse.

We feel incredibly pressured to see improvement in our clients. We are pressured by our clients and agencies, alike. But sometimes, our clients don't get better. Most times they do. *Better* rarely looks the way that we expect it to and is often difficult to identify. We have big ideas about what improvement means, and they are tragically flawed in their universality. No two *betters* look the same.

We often forget just how slow the change process is. We also forget that sometimes our clients shouldn't change their lives, but should grow more at peace within them. There is also a lot of frustration that comes with trying to make change. For domestic violence survivors, it usually takes eight tries before they are finally sincerely ready to leave their abusers. The diagnosis with the longest treatment time for recovery is anorexia, about seven to eight years. The frequency of relapse from drug and alcohol addiction is 75%.

Old habits die hard. But strong attachments yield long standing change. Strong attachments take time to build. We need to respect this. Most change is nonlinear. The idea of two steps forward and one step back almost always needs to be applied to our work. Go easy on yourself. Go easy on your clients. We are all trying when we have the energy to try. We are not in the "fix it" business and don't sell home improvement supplies, because they don't help the mind and soul. We need to be allowed to falter without feeling like we have failed. This goes for client and social worker alike.

To self-disclose or not?

There is tremendous anxiety and fear exerted around issues of self-disclosure. We spend many sessions debating about whether or not we should self-disclose. We spend other sessions regretting that we did self-disclose and promising ourselves that we won't tell anyone and we will never do it again. This is the thing about self-disclosure: it isn't THAT big of a deal. The anxiety associated with it and the significance of it are totally incongruent. We do self-disclose. Every time we get dressed in the morning, we are planning for multiple self-disclosures with the clothes we choose, the jewelry we wear, the fact that we may or may not wear makeup. It's okay. You are not supposed to shift the fact that this work is ultimately one real person sitting with another real person. You can't fight that fact and the inherent messiness that will come with it. The harder you fight it, the more ashamed of yourself and anxious you will become.

This is not work you can practice for or simulate in advance of a session, to feel more prepared. Our dress rehearsals are always the actual show. Sometimes we say too much; sometimes we say too little. Some of our interventions are more therapeutic than others. Most sessions are slow and unmemorable. Yet, some of the moments that we create, if we can shed our anxiety enough to be present for them, will be mutually magical and transformative.

Pink Tree

One of the greatest gifts of living in Philadelphia is that the cherry blossoms bloom in the spring. There is no way to get a bad picture of a cherry blossom tree. It almost feels like cheating. That said, I have long loved the effect of having a slight smudge on the screen of my camera that makes sunbeams look even more intense than they are in reality.

26. An Enactment With Rice— Reflections on Lunch and Therapy

I met Jane, the therapist of my life, in 1995. I was a sophomore in college, and I had just come out. I was working hard to stay afloat amidst the work of individuation, managing adult-like responsibilities, getting decent grades, and facing the truth of the chaotic family that I had left behind.

The vernacular around having a love of our life is well established. But we don't talk as much about the therapist of our life.

I had therapists before Jane, and I have had wonderful treatment after her, too—but none quite qualify as the therapist of my life in the same way. And I don't imagine anyone ever will. Like a first love, the spot is filled.

I had interviewed several therapists, most of them culturally familiar to me and archetypes of those I had long known, before finding my blond, blue-eyed, Connecticut-born, tall lesbian therapist. I decided that I wanted a therapist who did not remind me of my mother in any way. I certainly found her. She was confident, clear, and struck an unusual balance between kindness and bossiness.

I cancelled a session early on in our treatment for the "snow," and she told me that she was sure I could have made the walk and charged me for it. She was right. I could have. I was just playing my typical game of hide and seek, creating intense moments of intimacy and bowing out immediately after. She wasn't having any of it.

She kind of drove me crazy. I couldn't get enough. I tried to come in once a week; she said we needed twice. I tried to have my parents pay for the sessions; she said that the checks should be coming out of my own account. She wouldn't let me off easy for anything. While she took up a tremendous amount of space with her beliefs about the therapeutic frame, she also removed herself from the treatment in ways that were completely confounding for me. I asked her a million questions, all of which were met with the same response: "Well, what is your fantasy of what kind of car I have?"

Because I would unrelentingly invite her into an enactment, a repetitive form of interaction designed to recreate toxic and familiar dynamics, she had to remain incredibly steady. No matter how much someone had boundaries with me, I would push up against them. I would answer in whatever way I could to get the information that I wanted. I was always crafting answers strategically to collect data that would assure me that we could somehow fuse into one, rather than remaining and surviving between two separate people.

I would say that it would mean a lot to me if she had a Toyota, because it would give me a feeling of twinship, and I would have to work hard to understand if she had an American car, but I could probably accept it. I finally gave up and would just hang out in the parking lot of her office, trying to get the answers I wanted. I became a literal detective, tracking all the data about her life that I could find. It was pre-Google, but I still found her doctoral dissertation in the Columbia University library. The acknowledgments page was like straight porn for me.

Over the years, her protectiveness eased. As I gained insight about the excessive amounts of enmeshment in my family of origin, her need for a hard line softened. I also started to let myself know what I had come to know about her by just being in her presence for two 50-minute hours each week. I saturated several soothing pieces of knowledge—she was a Mac person, which at the time was sub-diagnostically subversive. She wore two different earrings, religiously, suggesting some bits of arrested development or just pure quirk. I came to know about her gayness by simply accepting my growing gaydar and the revealing tenor of her gender performance. While I still searched for her all around my college town on our non-session days, I calmed down a lot and simply started to take her in during our actual time together.

Taking her in changed me. I went from functioning in a way that aligns clearly with an anxious attachment and started to experience my relationships with a certain level of security and equilibrium. Instead of constantly feeling like I was going to be left or that someone I loved was going to die, unless awash in deep enmeshment, I began to discern based on my actual desires and burgeoning feelings of an actual self, shadowed with incubating feelings of self-respect.

In all of my detective work, I came across her home address one day. I held off on driving by before I finally surrendered to my insatiable curiosity. She had a sweet white house with black shutters and a basketball hoop in her driveway. Hanging over the fence of her front porch were wet kids' bathing suits and towels. I knew she had kids—this had come out over our time together. But the pedestrian representation of their safe and secure life with her was stirring. I confessed, of course. I could never hide anything from her. In the sharing, there was a recalibration of my understanding of her role in my developing psyche.

I told her that the idea of two little wet, chilled kids' bodies being wrapped in towels by her warm capable hands elicited searing desire in me. I wanted to be one of those kids. I wanted to have one of those kids myself one day. I wanted her as a mother, a model, a representation of what was possible within the confines of a predictable, parental system. I grieved for what I never had and feared for what I might not be able to create because of my own history of attachment ruptures and experiences of multiple forms of abuse by my narcissistic parents.

She told me that I could use the bathing suits, that it was okay to need to drive by and to take it all in as a symbol of my neglected childhood and as a possibility for my own future. She wasn't scared of my need for it and didn't make me feel gross for my needy scrutiny.

It always appeared to me that Jane deftly maneuvered her way around my standing invite into an enactment. If I wanted her to bend the treatment frame, she held it more firmly. If I wanted her to see me as the toxic stalker that I understood myself as, she helped me to re-see myself through kinder, gentler eyes. If I wanted her to reject me because of self-destructive life choices, she held me closer with authentic care and concern.

As our work ended, and I moved away from my safe college town, where I also completed graduate school, Jane and I embarked on a long, thoughtful, and curative termination. In our distance, I learned what it meant to have the presence of a relationship in soul and spirit. I learned that love didn't mean staying close, but sometimes moving toward one's goals and dreams. I also learned that I could see another therapist and this did not change the breadth or depth of our work together.

Perhaps two or three years after our final session, building my own career as a therapist, opening my own practice, Jane sent me a form letter saying that she was closing her practice. She was becoming a consultant to schools while I was renting my first space. We met to discuss this, and I asked her for her therapist chair. She said no. She said I needed a chair of my own. She was right. I was hurt. But I found my own chair for $765. Thirteen years later, I sit and hear the intricate stories of others hour after hour.

Thirteen years later, I also received an invitation to see Jane in my home city. She was coming to a conference and wondered if I wanted to meet. I suggested lunch, but I don't know why. She agreed. Her train was getting in at 2:00, and she would text me on her way. To say that every level of this interaction was vast departure from how we had been does not do the alien nature of it justice.

I texted a few hours before, insanely nervous and shaky, and suggested tea instead. She rebuked and said, "Let's stick with lunch." So, there I was, sitting at a table alone waiting for my waspy Connecticut, older therapist to arrive. I picked a Chinese restaurant, a cuisine that makes me feel at home. She gets dropped off by Uber, is wearing jeans, has a red rolling suitcase. I want a ginger ale to settle my stomach, but worry she will judge my sugar intake. I don't even know where that idiosyncratic fear is coming from.

She opens the menu and says that she hopes the restaurant has gluten-free options. She is gluten free? She lays her iPhone 6 Plus on the table. She has a 6 Plus, not a 6? She has an iPhone? Her 19-year-old son texts her during the meal. I peek to see what he has written. Her son texts her? She tells me that he has ADHD and is trying to make college work as much as he can. She tells me that her daughter is thinking about boarding school. She muses about the adolescents today and their addiction to electronic communication. I say almost nothing about my own kids, more than happy to step aside and eat her life up for lunch.

The curiosity, hunger, and desperation are as powerful as ever.

I tell her that sometimes I worry that I will run out of rice halfway through the meal. It is a long-standing anxiety of mine. No longer in the business of meaning making, she says, "Well, let's nip that in the bud and order another rice." I am soothed, but not really. Because it isn't about the rice, of course. We discuss how we will pay. She says she thought about it in advance and thinks that we should split it. Well, okay then. I hand her $40 cash, and she puts the whole amount on her card. The fact is that I paid more, but I always do, because that is another thing of mine that she is no longer studying.

> Once you order rice together, you can never go back.

I wait with her for the next Uber ride to her hotel. She texts me that she has arrived safely.

I drive home in aching pain, knowing that once you order rice together, you can never go back. Knowing that I will never have the space to process with her the overstimulation of all the tidbits that I collected about her life in the span of just about 92 minutes. Tidbits that would have taken years to learn about in the safe confines of her office, which had a turquoise iMac, soothing colors, and a revolving set of paintings that shifted with each season of our work. I cry, because I didn't even know she was taller than me until we were standing side by side for the first time.

Maybe I thought Jane was better at navigating enactments than she is. Or maybe enactments prevail despite our best efforts. When I say my family was unboundaried and enmeshed, I know that those words fall short of the sweeping reality of our ability to function as a fully fused unit, blind to the real human need for individuality and growth.

When I wanted to fuse with Jane all those years, perhaps she wanted the same. As I said, enactments are best understood as co-created. We had the therapeutic frame to hold the tremendous desire that I felt for her, but what about all the desire she may have felt for me? Did it all finally come out in a text about meeting because of a randomly scheduled and geographically located conference? And will ordering an extra rice ever actually make me feel less of a scarcity of relational resources? I don't know.

I do know that we have no more 50-minute hours left to find the answers to these questions. I also know that I won't ever have lunch with one of my patients. But I will do other things that enact their deepest fears, which will only be remedied by the fact of my office, my chair, and our 50-minute hours together.

PART 5
On Theory

Banality

This picture feels like a quintessential representation of what photography has taught me. Art and others' attention to detail is all
around us. On the corks alone, you see tremendous effort and the
labor of love. The attention to these small objects drowns out, in-
tentionally, the grandness of the world outside. This is what micro
focus can gift us with, the possibility of seeing what is right in front
of us rather than being dwarfed by all that can thwart our efforts.

27. Joining the Chorus

A client of mine who is revisiting a lifelong passion of hers after years of fear and ambivalence asked me, "Will I always hate myself? Will this voice of hatred always be here?" It's a good question.

A few days later in a supervision group that I run, a relatively new social worker was talking about the enduring feelings of shame that she feels in her job because she has "bad boundaries." She wonders if the shame will ever go away. Will she ever feel as if her boundaries are good enough? It's a good question.

In both instances, which are really two mere examples of psychic states that we all share, I feel an internal debate about how to respond. I want to say, "Of course you will stop hating yourself," or "Of course you will start to feel more confident about your boundaries." I think about the strengths perspective, about the role of hope, about the power of unconditional positive regard, and the answers are so clear. Yes, relief will come.

But will it really? In many ways, I don't actually think so. The reason that I know the real answer to this question is because of my own experience of living within the environment of my mind. I feel self hatred all the time. I question my boundaries all the time, too. Even in writing this, there are constant questions and fears about being too much, about saying too much, about not knowing what to write. Yet I am writing this and risking putting myself out there, despite the fear.

Therein lies the answer to the questions. Yes, there is a part of me that hates myself. Yes, there is a part of me that questions my own boundaries. But those are parts of me, voices in a larger chorus. The goal, I believe, in our work with our clients, is not to stop the self hatred, but to diversify the internal experience that they have of themselves.

A powerful concept in object relations theory is related to the idea of *introjects*. It is argued that introjects are internalized messages taken in from early attachment figures that configure the way we have come to understand ourselves. For my patient, her mother loved her but also felt incredibly overwhelmed by her. She is a twin and was often aware (on some level) of her mother's feeling that she couldn't handle both of her babies. This manifested into a sense of self hatred that still sustains itself today, particularly when my client is stressed out, depleted, and lacking internal or external resources.

> Our work is to join the chorus, providing an alternate tune or melody.

Our work as clinical social workers is not necessarily to compete with the introjects, although we sometimes do. But wrestling matches are often hard fought, losing battles. Instead, our work is to join the chorus, providing an alternate tune or melody. Perhaps, we are the soprano to the towering alto. Bear with me—I am a horrible singer myself and basically tone deaf. But I am a decent writer and also really good at parallel parking. See, my work is not to become a good singer (that simply won't happen); it is to become more than a bad singer.

I once had a supervisor tell me that it was not important to hate or love our clients, but instead that we ought to hate and love our clients *properly*. This is a powerful notion. I can't just say to my client, "Your mother was totally overwhelmed by you, but I am not." I can't just become the alternate introject. It isn't that simple. This is partly because my client may actually be overwhelming.

Instead, we need to shift the introject's hold by discovering with our clients that they are more than one thing. My client can be overwhelming, but she isn't only that. She is also unbelievably smart and passionate. When I am making food for my picky children, I often find myself thinking that this client would know what to do. She has a way of understanding the complexity of both children and food that I envy. This is the truth. And that is one of many truths that help me to love her properly, precisely, and authentically. It gives me a legitimate place on a crowded stage.

It is with that love, the specificity and idiosyncratic nature of it, that I can become another introject. As you can imagine, her mother had the tendency to sing solo with some other bit parts played by siblings, her father, grandparents, and perhaps a teacher or two. The more voices in the chorus, the less powerful any one of them can be. The hope in bringing about a chorus of voices is to aid our clients in ultimately auditioning for their own solo, sung in their own voice.

Back to the supervisee and the shame. Part of the reason that I mention her struggle alongside that of my client's is that there is a wholly false dichotomy in our perception around who has these struggles. It isn't just our clients. It is all of us. We all dwell in shame, self hatred, and doubt. The question is how we can keep these introjects, these self states, from becoming paralyzing or defining. By sharing her shame in group supervision, my supervisee is offered a nearly literal chorus. The fellow social workers in the group echoed their resonance with this fear and pain. However, they also countered with their real experiences of my supervisee, knowing that her astute clinical insight and capacity for self reflection are also essential parts of her melody and must be played, at least alongside (if not louder than) the painful song of uncertainty.

28. Boundaries Versus the Super Ego

I am often struck by the complex anxiety that we share, as social workers, around creating boundaries. It is, of course, of exquisite importance to maintain solid boundaries in our clinical work. However, it often feels as if our wish to remain boundaried becomes conflated with a real and paralyzing fear that somehow we will be transgressive. This fear can keep us from being authentically present in our clinical interactions. In fact, I would argue that this fear is often more driven by the superego, which can act punitively and shamefully, than by our ego, which can act thoughtfully and carefully.

A bit of background

Let me take a second for some background. Our clinical work is basically founded upon Sigmund Freud's principle of the "talking cure." Although Freud was not a social worker, his findings and theories loom large in our conceptualization of our own work. He argued that psychological relief comes from the articulation of our thoughts and feelings through language. More specifically, he argued that, through free association, we would be able to access our more inner, unconscious thoughts and bring them to the surface in the presence of an objective and benevolent listener—the clinician.

He was extremely concerned with boundaries and essentially called for the banishment of the clinician's subjective experience from the clinical encounter—hoping for nearly antiseptic and neutral clinicians. He warned, beginning in 1913, that the more we, as clinicians, become involved in the treatment, the more dangerous the treatment can become.

While we are haunted by Sigmund Freud's (the father) warnings, we are often less exposed to the very powerful role of his daughter, Anna. Anna was his sixth child. She became a social worker and spent most of her time working closely with children in nurseries, bringing about the movement toward child psychoanalysis. She worked humanely and accessibly with her clients. In other words, she operated from her ego. Not an inflated ego, but a balanced, analytic, and thoughtful one.

Sigmund articulated the very resonant idea of the tripartite mind. He said that we have an *id, ego,* and *superego.* He warned, of course, of the dangers of the id—the center for drive and aggression. He also probably did quite a bit, through the creation of his theory, to place us deeply in the realm of our superego as we practice. He believed that therapists might seek gratification from their clients and collapse the boundaries in the service of that. He, in fact, had very little faith in the safety of our egos, as clinicians. Ironically, what is less covered is the fact that he analyzed his own daughter, a certain collapse of boundaries and ego functioning. While he left us to panic as we battle our superegos, his own grandiosity (or id) led him to incredible transgressions.

We cannot remain completely neutral.

Because it is essentially impossible to remain completely neutral, sterile, or objective, our attempts to do so fail. When our attempts fail, we fear that we are becoming unboundaried and, therefore, bad. Really bad, in fact. And our superegos remind us of this over and over again, leaving us in a spiral of shame and loneliness.

I recently had a student discuss a process recording of a final session with a client she deeply cared about. Her client was getting ready to move away for new and promising adventures. My student, the clinician, felt ashamed of how sad she felt about the pending separation between them, but didn't want to say anything. She wanted to make sure that she didn't make the session about her. She wanted to make sure that her client didn't feel guilty or responsible for making her upset. So, they parted ways and her very subjective experience of attachment, sadness, and pride in her client's accomplishments was never shared dyadically.

Is this a case of good boundaries? I don't know. I think it is a case of complex super ego functioning. My student became scared that if she were to authentically enter the room, she wouldn't be able to control herself. She became scared that if she were to authentically enter the room, this would somehow eclipse the amount of space that her client could occupy.

In between presence and absence

The fact is that there has to be something in between presence and absence. Further, the shame we feel about how we feel about our clients is not only about boundaries. It is also about the stark vulnerability that comes with attachment. The truth is that we get attached to our clients, and they can leave us at any time. While they may fear being abandoned by us, the success of our work is measured by their eventual abandonment of us. The better we do, the more likely we are to be left.

We need to try and imagine a space between boundary violations and the mythology of neutrality. A space where we take risks. Without this imagination, we start to feel silenced and afraid. With it, we can become creative, balanced, and enlivened. What if my student had said to her client, "I am so sad to see you go, but so amazed by the depths of the work you have done and excited for how prepared you are for the next chapter"? Or, "It is hard to see you go, but I wouldn't want it any other way, because this is a testament to your growth and your health"?

Central questions

How do you know if you are operating out of respect for boundaries or out of punitive superego functioning? Or if you are just avoiding your own fear of abandonment? I think that these are central questions that we need to keep asking ourselves. I also think there are some answers. If we can show up in a way that is transparent, premeditated, and careful, I believe we can be with our clients in a brave, important, boundaried, and honest way. If we show up in a way that is impulsive, seeking some sort of internal gratification, and feels internally unwise, then I think we are in the realm of transgression.

The clinical frame and our code of ethics

We also have the beautiful support of the clinical frame, whatever that may be. It may be that you meet in a certain office, at a certain time, for a specific duration of time. The frame is designed to contain transgression while allowing for bountiful clinical exploration and possibility. We also have the beautiful support of the *Code of Ethics*. We aren't to barter, create dual relationships, or experience physical intimacy. This code exists to contain transgression while allowing for the bountiful possibility of emotional intimacy, the exploration of trauma, and the experience of real attachment.

The fact is that our roots are grounded in complex family dynamics, specifically those between Anna (a social worker and a daughter) and Sigmund Freud (a neurologist and a father), among many others, I am sure. In many ways, this has left us with the intergenerational feeling of shame and residue. It has also provided us with a lot of valuable theory and guiding thought. Within this, however, we must find our own idiosyncratic mode of truly being with our clients in ways that honor interdependence, vulnerability, and trust that the mutual articulation of attachment can be survived.

Boundaries don't have to equal withholding silence, and truly showing up is not a transgression. Our superegos need not be our guide. Our clinical frames and professional ethics more than suffice.

29. It's Not You, It's Me

I had a client come in the other day saying that she's not sure about how she is feeling about our work together. She said that sometimes when she leaves a session, she starts to feel unclear about what is coming from her mind and what is coming from my mind. She went on to say that she feels like our "energy gets all mixed together." She is articulating a powerful reality of how this all can feel by speaking to the pain of trying to delineate between a pair of subjectivities—her subjectivity versus mine, my subjectivity versus hers.

> Any clinical dyad paves the way toward a mutual psychological experience, a merging of each player's past and present.

We have long been taught that the clinical relationship is based on the client as the psychological centerpiece. Although this notion sustains its importance, it was falsely supported by the fantasy of a social worker's clinical objectivity. It was believed that the social worker could remain neutral enough to contain, reflect, and support the clients' arrival at their own truths, struggles, and insights. As we have come to realize, this neutrality is a false construct that is essentially impossible to achieve. Further, the idea of a dyad constructed of an object and a subject has been replaced by the understanding of a mutually built and co-created inter-subjectivity. When my client said that she can't tell our minds apart, perhaps she was on to something.

I had another client who felt wounded by a recent report given to her by a psychologist based on weeks of psychological testing—everything from Rorschach to IQ tests. It offered up some negative conclusions about her character structure that led her to rethink her idea about who she is. I offered up the possibility that the tester/psychologist was a subjective actor who wrote the report. Although the tests are presumably valid and reliable, the tester always confounds the findings by bringing that individual's own subjectivity to the interpretation of the findings. This brought tremendous relief to her as she realized, of course, the natural fallacy that accompanies any practitioner's humanity.

The whole issue of subject and subject versus subject and object becomes toxic in two predictable ways. The first occurs when a subject/social worker claims a level of positivistic objectivity that can leave a client feeling crazy and alone. The other occurs when a subject/social worker claims the fact of being subjective, but insists that there is some level of righteousness to that perception (because of experience or training) that leaves the client feeling like the subjugated student to the clinician's supposed expertise and teachings.

If we can claim the fact and struggle of our intersubjectivity, the coming together of two minds, the important work of sorting out who is who and what is what can begin to happen.

Sandor Ferenczi (1919), Jessica Benjamin (2004), and Thomas Ogden (1994) have all worked to name the power of intersubjective work, mutuality, mutual transformation, and the co-creation of psychic spaces. Ferenczi called it "mutual analysis," Benjamin calls it "thirdness," and Ogden calls it "the analytic third." What all three were trying to say is that any clinical dyad paves the way toward a mutual psychological experience, a merging of each player's past and present coupled with the historic tendencies toward transference and countertransference.

My client who leaves confused said that she sometimes feels she goes too far in her anger toward her husband when we are sitting together. She feels almost inauthentic in her presentation of their dynamic, making their marriage sound much darker than it actually is. And accordingly, when I hear her talk, I start to feel this weird wish for her to consider leaving him. I call the wish "weird" because it feels sort of displaced and misattuned. I think about my past, long-standing wish for my parents to get divorced, although they never did, and how this must be playing out in our work.

Perhaps my unconscious wish for my childhood to have been different is interacting with her unconscious wish to please—a relic from her childhood patterns.

There are so many ways this inferno could blow if I were unwilling to take responsibility for my part in it. At the same time, if I were to take sole responsibility for my role in it, she would be left off the hook with nothing of her own disavowed process to make sense of. So, I take a risk to bring myself into the room, to remove myself from the room enough for her to reconnect with her own inner world. It sounds tricky. And it is. I say to her, "I do think that sometimes we go to extreme places about him. I think that part of this is my stuff. At the same time, I wonder if any of it feels like it authentically belongs to you? What I do know is that, though it might not seem like it, I never think of your husband in one dimension. I realize that we are just sifting through pieces of a complex person."

In my response, I am taking some responsibility. I am reassuring her that my perception is more complex than I might be portraying. And, I am inviting her in subjectivity. The truth is that there is no real way to ever precisely separate her mind from my mind. There is no clear path to exactly compartmentalize who thinks and feels what. But through transparency, we can start to clear things up.

Also, by recognizing what happens when the two of us are together, we give voice to the "thirdness" that arises in our work. Giving voice to this thirdness allows the therapist to properly exit stage left, recreating the authentic possibility of the client psyche as ultimate centerpiece.

Micro-Flower

One of the easiest pictures that someone can take is a close-up of a flower. The more closely that a flower is studied, the more beautiful it becomes. It has the power to put everything around it to shame. This flower is at my house and, despite the size of my house, it is bigger and more beautiful in every way.

30. On Couples

Whether you work with couples or you work with individuals, the fact is that you work with couples in some capacity. This is because most of our clients bring in their most intimate relationships, either literally or psychically. To practice clinical social work successfully, it is essential to have a clear sense of the underlying psychological themes that both haunt and strengthen couples.

Do opposites attract?

We have all heard the age-old adage that opposites attract. For some it seems true, and for others, of course, it does not. The fact is that there is something to the idea of why people form intimate relationships. Part of the reason that opposites attract is that having a partner who has the capacity for something that we do not offers us containment. For example, half of a couple might be able to apologize, half of a couple might not fly toward anger, half of a couple might be incredibly social. The reason that these characteristics might feel attractive to someone who holds the opposite trait is that it offers the possibility of containing a part of us that we fear or a part of us that feels underdeveloped. The person who can't apologize, on some level, wishes that they could and envies the person who has the ego strength to survive apologizing. The person who flies toward anger often envies the person who maintains calm and equanimity.

We are drawn to something in someone that we wish we had, that we wish we could develop. Relationship problems start to arise when the couple starts to become entrenched in their roles, relying solely on the strength of one partner and never working toward developing these capacities in the psyche of the other. When working with couples, it is useful to assess the level of exhaustion that accompanies an overreliance on one person's capacity for something, while the other couple member gets to remain stuck in what is hard for that member. Couples who are able to survive need to work to better distribute the emotional labor. This usually requires a retracing of what originally drew them to each other and seeing if these traits can be more evenly split between both partners.

Projective identification

Along with seeking containment for the parts of us that feel un-wieldy or immaturely developed, we also use our partner's psyche to regulate parts of our own emotional world. Let's think about how often we hear about people who hate their mothers-in-law. It is an al-most iconic image—the husband who never wants his mother-in-law to visit and stay for more than a day, or the wife who is gritting her teeth as she is listening to her mother-in-law critique how a meal has turned out.

These images are iconic because of something called *projective identification*. A member of the couple has psychological experiences that feel intolerable. This experience becomes disavowed, but it is kept alive in the psyche of the partner. For example, a daughter feels angry at her mother, knows she needs space from her, and is uncon-sciously wishing to individuate. Because these feelings are intolerable, the daughter invites her mother for a visit instead of dealing with her uncomfortable and threatening emotions. She converts these feelings into the inverse experience of them. This is a defense called *reaction formation*. But feelings never disappear unless they are confronted somehow. The intimate partner of the daughter starts expressing dis-comfort and rage about the visit, and the conflict becomes lodged in the wrong dyad—between the partners rather than between the mother and daughter.

This is a complicated psychological process that underlies a tre-mendous number of struggles between couples. A member of the cou-ple will take on the unbearable, psychic material of the partner. The partner then becomes enraged at the person taking on these feelings, as if it is an affront to them. A large part of our work, in understand-ing couples, is to help couples to reclaim and reassign emotions to their original incubator, the mind that is struggling with the content. When these feelings are properly reclaimed, metabolized, and man-aged in the originating psyche, the burden of this process is taken off the couple, and authentic dyadic functioning can resume.

Surrendering objectivity

The seductive power of seeking objectivity when working with couples is titillating. When sitting with a couple or with an individual, we are invariably drawn to determine who is truly at fault. When vio-lence is present, this is quite important to do. But most of the time, struggles between couples are co-created. Each member of the couple has a subjective experience. They turn to us hoping for some objectiv-ity, for someone to see the "truth." The fact is that in a relationship, there is no actual, fundamental truth. Instead, our constant search, along with the members of the couples, is to search, search, search, for how every single dynamic is co-created. We might hear about how one member of the couple never cleans, never takes care of the kids, never contacts extended family. Although these symptoms seem to reveal clear fault, that level of simplistic understanding is problematically reductive. The question needs to become, "Well, why do you keep cleaning if your partner doesn't?" We need to help clients recognize how they are equal partners in replenishing repetitive dynamics.

Our search for objectivity ought to be replaced by the knowledge that the mere presence of a fresh outlook might help couple members to re-see what has become un-seeable. Couple members start to experience their patterns of functioning as inevitable. Our presence, the mere fact of it, shifts them away from this perception of inevitability by our offering alternate, empathic perspectives on their struggles.

Repetitive templates

All couple members come to relationships with past experiences of intimate relationships—with siblings, past partners, parents. These early attachments become imprinted in our minds and form expectancies about how our current and future relationships will play out. Recognizing and articulating these templates that have become imprints, we assist individuals in spotting the ways their psyches anticipate and therefore manifest relational outcomes. When clients are stressed and lacking internal resources for a whole host of reasons (stretched finances, struggles with kids, problems at work), they are more likely to rely upon the information they have come to know from their pasts, rather than what is happening in front of them. For each member of a couple to internalize the actual stimuli of the current relationship, a psychological clearing needs to be made.

Clinically, our work is to help individuals and couples to create this exact clearing, so they can engage with the partner in front of them, rather than the partners who are long behind them. Keeping clients engaged in the present often requires a certain honoring, but not succumbing to, the past. This is one of the many ways in which work with clients requires us to remain balanced and unassuming. We are dealing with ghosts, ghost stories, and competing new fictions and non-fictions. Finding a way through all of this requires a total surrender to the complexity of the couple relationship, along with a knowledge that there are also lovingly simple ways out of what appears deceivingly impossible.

PART 6
Self-Care

Horizon

I recently started to go to something that I like to call "writing school." What I mean is that I am in my first year of a program at the Washington School for Psychoanalysis on writing. I take the train to Washington from Philadelphia and stare at the Chesapeake Bay's shifting presentation of the horizon.

31. Social Workers as Empaths, Small Talk, and Self-Preservation

My therapist (a social worker) and I (a social worker) were discussing how hard it is to make friends in adulthood. I was talking about my long summer of visits to the swim club, feeling proud of how many people I know there. Yet, I struggle with how to make conversation, otherwise known as small talk. The ease with which everyone is communicating startles me, as I envy some sort of social expertise they all seem to have. My social worker therapist hypothesized that perhaps this is an occupational hazard. And I agree with her hypothesis.

The reason, I think, is that many times, social workers are social workers because they were already empaths. And if the egg didn't give birth to the chicken, then let's also say that social workers often *become* empaths once enough souls have been bared to them.

Empaths are people who feel with exquisite precision, are quite vulnerable to absorbing the energy of those around them, are easily hurt, are often considered "over-sensitive," cannot easily compartmentalize psychological experiences, are innately intuitive, and have excessive access to the emotional lives of those around them.

Because there is such a high overlap between empaths and social workers, I thought it would be helpful to consider part of how being an empath-social worker has an impact on our overall lives. I also want to give voice to the reality of how we, social worker-empaths, negotiate the significant psychological residue of our daily lives.

Secret families

As social worker-empaths, we take our clients' lives and minds deeply into our own. We often sit with clients and develop the capacity to not only anticipate their feelings, but experience so much of their emotional lives with them. In some ways, it can feel as if our clients live inside our minds. In other ways, it can feel as if we even keep our clients alive by thinking about them, internalizing them, and remaining curious about them. It can even feel like our clients are part of our family—our psychological family, at least.

The weird part about having our clients as tenants in our minds, our family members in our souls, is that this all happens in secret. Perhaps our supervisors know, or a few of our colleagues know, but no one *really* knows the way that our clients constellate in our minds. Because of this, we sift through holidays, dinner dates, even food shopping, in this odd dualistic stance. We are present with the people we are with (sometimes), but are engaged with our clients in a way that can feel invisible and isolating.

The idea of having two families can almost feel akin to having a biological family and an adoptive one. We are fully committed to one, but our mind wanders to the other, quite privately and quietly.

Small talk

When we ask a client, upon our first meeting, "How are things at home?" we know and our clients know what we mean. We mean: *Are you being abused? Are you happy? Are you telling the truth? Do you feel lied to? Do you feel safe?* When we are with our friends and we say, "How are things at home?" we usually hear: "Fine. How are things with you?" And the expected response, of course, is, "Oh, good." The fact that our language can mean such different things across distinct settings is downright disorienting. How can we adjust?

If we are social worker-empaths, the fact is that we can't. We are much more comfortable speaking a deeper language, a truer language. We feel, often, most at ease with our clients' complex responses. We feel, often, most at ease with hearing unfolding stories tethered together by intricate traumas and intergenerational patterns of attachment and pain. To function across spheres, we either need to master some sort of code switching or feel lonely a lot of the time. Or both.

The fact is that social workers are not great at small talk. We excel at relationship construction, but the stuff of swim clubs, baby showers, and happy hour can feel excruciatingly elusive and odd.

Powerful antennae

Of course, another reason why small talk can be so hard is that every time we hear someone say, "I'm fine," we know how much is being obscured by the niceties and superficiality. Part of the pain of functioning as a social worker-empath in the world is that we walk around with powerful antennae that make us feel what others are feeling, see things that others aren't seeing, and feel a good amount of what is psychologically disavowed by communities around us.

For example, we have all habituated (at least somewhat) to walking past a homeless person on the street. But when we do it, it certainly doesn't feel simple. First, we access all of our clients' stories and see them in that person on the street. Second, we know the socioeconomic complexity of their struggle and understand the way that micro and macro factors have colluded to leave them on the street. We also struggle to bear witness to the others who are just walking by, feeling alone in the depths of our own effort to just move on.

It can feel like our antennae become overstimulated and overwrought. We can tune in to so many signals at one time that it can feel deafening. It can also feel crazy-making when we *know* that many around us are not perceiving reality in this rough and textured way. We can feel crazy, oversensitive, and frankly kind of ridiculous. We are often left envying the capacity of others to move through the world with seeming ease while we muddle across streets in unsettling disease.

We also can feel burdened by the ways in which our friends and family make use of us, relying on our antennae, to help them self-regulate. The fact is that many share things with us that they don't share with others. We are often burdened by keeping secrets for others, seeing the truth of seemingly simple dynamics, or just knowing that everything happens in systemic contexts, rendering us constantly assessing. We feel left holding an undue amount of information, while others feel the relief of not tuning in.

Self-preservation

There is tremendous buy-in to the concepts of extroversion and introversion. There is substantial validity in the fact of these identities. At the same time, the social worker-empath doesn't necessarily fall squarely under either heading. We find great comfort in being with others, at times. At others, it is incredibly taxing. We find great comfort in being alone, at times. At others, it is incredibly taxing. Our level of introversion or extroversion is measured by the psychological-mindedness of those around us. If we are around others who seem to really "get it," the relief is endless and energizing. If we are around others who seem particularly misattuned, our tanks can feel as if they are leaking, leaving us solidly empty.

We can feel burdened even by Facebook, as we witness the multiple ways in which people perform "fine" and "good" and "happy" and "perfect." The fact is that social worker-empaths are often left feeling crazy and tired. The need for self-preservation with others (the right ones) or alone (at the right times) is uniquely essential, given how sensitive our systems are to external stimuli and painful data.

I wish that social workers could talk more openly with each other about all of this. Maybe some of you do. But I don't think it is easy. We habituate to keeping things to ourselves; the rules of confidentiality support us in doing that.

Perhaps we can all come out as more real, lonely, saturated, and enlivened by all that we do and the elaborate ways in which we experience it all.

32. The Tyranny of Self Help or the Necessity of Existential Depression

My son struggles with sensory processing disorder. He does not seek sensory stimuli. Instead, he typically avoids it because the experience of "too much" of anything is extremely hard for him to take. In other words, he experiences the world in a deep way and he needs help not taking it all in so intensely.

Irvin Yalom (1981) wrote about near necessity of an existential depression. He suggested that a certain level of depression is normal, if not essential. He suggested that this depression is the byproduct of negotiating some key elements of our world and lives. These elements are death, freedom, isolation, and meaninglessness. He argued that the inner conflict that arises in negotiating these forces leaves us depressed and disillusioned.

The fact of mass shootings and community violence continues to unfold at an unrelenting pace. I don't yet know where or when the next shooting will be, but I will soon. We all will. Then we will subsequently un-know it, so we can go on and manage our lives and psyches. Yalom argued, in many ways, that the "going on" that we do is the real pathology. And the depression that would slow us down is a sign of our health, our true cognitive dissonance in the face of a world that makes less and less sense all the time.

So, as my son is working on becoming less sensitive, I wonder if we need to be doing the opposite, for ourselves and for our clients. What if we can't shake it? What if we can't go on? Wouldn't that be truly healthy?

I had a client describe her fetishization of self-help. I found that term fascinating and incredibly spot-on. The self-help industry sets up social work for failure by dangling the illusion of ultimate inner peace and sustainable calm. You can buy a book about how to get rid of everything in your home. You can buy a book about exactly what to buy for your home to make your home perfect. You can buy a book about how to connect with your inner creative goddess. You can buy a book about creating the perfect meditation practice. You can buy a book about how juicing will cleanse you so you will never feel fat again. And you can read all of those books and wonder why you still aren't well. And then you will probably feel like you should have bought a different book, a more "right" book.

The fact is that there is a level of discomfort and pain, a level of sensitivity, that perhaps we should not remove ourselves from. And we certainly shouldn't keep trying to remove our clients from it. Self-help offers the possibility of individual relief from intrapsychic strife. But the truth is that the world is far more unwell than any one of our clients. As we enable the idea that the resolution to un-wellness can reside in any one psyche, we become more dishonest. Yes, we want to provide psychic relief. Yes, we want to bolster functionality. But there is also a certain dysfunction to functioning through the world as we currently know it.

So, then what? What if we embrace dysfunction and depression? What if we refuse the dangling carrot of the self-help section at Barnes and Noble? What if we don't try to make our clients feel less pain than they do at any given moment?

> **What if we refuse the dangling carrot of the self-help section at Barnes and Noble? What if we don't try to make our clients feel less pain than they do at any given moment?**

Well, then I think that we are in the true heart of our work. I think we are in at least one of the four chambers that pumps the blood through the body of what we were founded upon. There are a few things that I think separate our work from all the rest. The NASW calls these things: service, social justice, dignity and worth of the person, importance of human relationships, integrity, and competence.

I agree, yet I might word it differently. I call these things: the refusal to sit idly by while innocent community members are gunned down, the refusal to pretend that it is all okay when the distribution of wealth in this country has become literally abusive, the refusal to diagnose homeless veterans with paranoid schizophrenia when they return to a country that has no place for them to rest their heads or to earn a paycheck, the refusal to think of a drug addict as a criminal. I could go on.

When my clients come in tomorrow and are feeling scared and sad, I will be scared and sad, too. I will be scared and sad with them. And the ones who are not scared and sad are the ones who I will more seriously worry about.

Maybe my son's appointment will make him a little less sensitive because he will practice ways of integrating sensory processes. But I hope it doesn't desensitize him too much, because we need as much sensitivity as we can get to decide what we are going to do. Because we have to do something.

33. Self-Care During Resolution Season

I personally get extremely overwhelmed during the transition to the New Year. I become saturated by the feeling that I should be doing everything differently. I don't know where to start. The worst part is that as the year winds down, I find myself becoming increasingly complacent with some of my most self-destructive ways of being, because I have this strong fantasy of how things will become magically better when the New Year comes.

I know that nothing that I am saying sounds unfamiliar. We are all in this cycle. It is a cycle largely fueled by capitalism, which is bolstered by selling more and more to convince us that betterment can be purchased. It is a large machine that can be nearly abusive to our psyches. It also negates the very real and sustaining truth that we are often in a good enough state that requires very little tweaking.

As clinical social workers, though, the tweaking that we do need to attend to is *self-care*. This is true throughout the year, and that has nothing to do with New Year's resolutions. It cannot be secured through any purchases or subscriptions or memberships, particularly the ones that are on sale starting January 1st.

Self-care for us is different than it is for many other professionals. We don't just need a vacation every 6-8 weeks. A mental health day offers a certain reset, but not a sustainable one. Finding sustainable paths to self-care, in our field, takes the effort to recognize our own idiosyncratic needs and the ways in which *we* are left with the overwhelming residue of our work.

I want to preface this by saying that I don't feel like an expert at self-care in any way. In fact, I feel I am pretty bad at it. That said, I feel there are some ways in which I have come to understand how to maximize support, understand myself professionally, and to talk to others about their cases in a way that provides relief.

You get hurt.

When I started to do dissertation research, I was interviewing experienced therapists about their experience of loving their clients. I learned a tremendous amount, but there is something that someone said to me that stuck. He said: "Before we end the interview, I want to tell you one thing: it's that you get hurt. You get hurt by your clients, and no one tells you that." Now, a decade later, I cannot believe how true these words are. We are frequently armed with the powerful reminder to "do no harm." Problematically, though, we spend less time learning about and preparing for the ways in which we get harmed.

We meet with clients who have strongly avoidant attachment styles, complex trauma histories, inconsistent patterns of relating, and often regulate their own self esteem through the diminishing of others. We ourselves get diminished. We get hurt. We are abandoned (often without explanation). I once had a client tell me that I was talking about myself too much when she asked me how I was doing and I said that I was getting over a cold. I had another client make fun of the place where I went on my honeymoon (although she didn't know that I had gone there) because it didn't compare to an island she had been to in Hawaii. I had a client who was at a meeting where I was being discussed, and he told me how some of the people there didn't like me.

It gets complicated. We can't just tell our clients that they hurt us. It's not that simple. We need to give them the space to interact in ways that are authentic to who they are, and this is often sloppy. But we can't just disappear, either. Part of our work, in terms of self-care, is honoring the part of us that gets hurt by our clients. Sometimes we find ways to say something to our clients that is productive; a lot of times we don't.

So what do we do with the hurt parts of ourselves? A key part of self-care on the part of the clinical social worker is to surrender the shame that comes from having feelings induced by our clients. There is so much written about the professional stance, objectivity, and clearing ourselves of countertransference. But that makes it very hard to just admit that we are hurt. Admitting that we are hurt is a huge piece of taking care of ourselves. We can admit it to a friend, a co-worker, or a supervisor. Those are huge steps. But those steps don't compare to how essential it is to remain open to the truth of our vulnerability in this work. Without recognizing that utter vulnerability, our capacity for woundedness, abandonment, and disappointment, we cannot properly care for ourselves.

You aren't talking about your work too much.

I am sure that most of you, if not all, feel as if when you are talking about your work, you are talking about it too much. You aren't. I say that having no idea how much you are talking about it, and I am still sure that I am right. To do clinical social work well, your brain is probably working overtime to process the multitude of complex dynamics that you see on a daily basis. We are always walking the tightrope that hovers right above micro and macro, intrapsychic and interpersonal, theoretical orientations, agency politics, and ethical decision-making.

The multiple levels of thought that this work requires likely means that your mind is racing a lot of the time. My hunch is that you articulate 1-2% of your internal processes aloud. This takes the steam off what can feel like a psychological pressure cooker. We *need* to talk to process. Oftentimes, we need to talk a lot and that still doesn't quite take the sharp edge off the scary terrain we navigate. To take care of yourself, you must talk and you must find places to talk and people to talk to. The shame you feel about talking too much must be understood as a parallel process. Most of our clients feel like "too much," too. But by risking telling our stories and taking up space with them, we are helping our clients to do the same, by clearing out our storage areas for them to more safely occupy.

You are good enough.

When Winnicott talked about the good enough mother, he was, of course, also referencing the good enough therapist and the good enough social worker. He argued, thoughtfully, that all we need to be good enough is "simple patience." Asserting that health can only be achieved when clients arrive at their own answers, Winnicott suggested that providing a predictable, reliable, and warm holding environment would elicit the growth necessary for clients to become more authentically themselves. What this means is that we never have to have the answers. We spend so much time trying to figure out the right thing to say, the right thing to do. The fact is that, oftentimes, the less we do, the more "good" we are. I hear so many supervisees say, "But I don't feel like I am doing anything." And my answer, which is how I am providing for the possibility of self-care through self-talk, is: "Exactly, keep not doing anything." In a moment when we are pressured by measurable outcomes, action steps, and endless goal setting, something about the magic of our work is lost. Self-care is a true returning to the simple essence of our work: to tolerate the not-knowing stance in the presence of others who doubt that they can ever find the answers within.

The problem with resolutions

The idea of resolutions and why they conflict so much with actual self-care is that they are resolute, clear, black and white. Nothing that we do falls under this heading. We can have a client remain deeply attached to an abusive attachment figure and feel that we have failed, because the outcome lacks resolution. Our work as clinical social workers is to resist the temptation of resolution, knowing that simplicity rarely comes when we are talking about human suffering. My work in terms of self-care is to surrender my wish for a client to seek a clear resolution, clear relief, an ending to pain. Instead, I remember that my clinical success is largely measured by my own ability to tolerate the ambiguity of my clients' choices and to help them tolerate the ambiguity of their own lives. Self-care is the embracing of ambiguity and the rejection of the possibility for resolution.

Talk more, let yourself be hurt, and know that we are all unsure about what we are doing. The self-care takes shape when we connect to ourselves and others around those exquisite realities.

34. Art as Self-Care, The Art of Self-Care

In 2016, I took a picture of a windmill, at night, in the snow. I took the picture with my phone. It was no big deal, no real investment of time, and certainly no investment of money.

I have always struggled with the idea of self-care. It isn't that I don't know how to do it; it is that I often feel like I can't afford it. It is also that I can never find the time. In some ways, the idea of self-care has felt like more work. But when I took that one picture, I noticed something. It was this tiny glow of a yellow floodlight near the bottom of the windmill. The light shined on it and on the snow. It made the snow look like this soft, pale yellow. It also made the windmill look like it was alive. Just a tiny moment of magic.

I decided, that night, that I would start taking pictures daily. I would not spend a lot of time on it, and I would not spend any money on a camera. I would just use what I had. These feel like powerful parts of what might make self-care possible for me. Minimal effort, maximum reward.

As I write this, it has been more than 400 days since I began taking pictures. I tried first to take pictures of things that were meaningful and somehow significant. For instance, I was always searching for intense moments of juxtaposition and paradox, like litter next to trash bins. Then I realized that I was working too hard for it. I was bringing the same intensity to my art that I bring to my work. The beauty of art is that it requires a certain surrendering, an unthinking. The same is true of self-care. It should not require concentrated effort. Instead, it should call upon more underused muscles of ours, relaxed ones that force a renunciation of exertion.

There are some days when I don't want to take a picture. But I force myself to. It feels kind of unnatural and weird, but I still think that it is important. When we are most depleted, self-care is the hardest. This is why creating a habit out of it makes it potentially healing in a more sustainable manner. We need to try and create self-care even when we feel we don't need it. On the days when I don't feel like taking a picture, I find an amazing moment of light reflecting on the river by

Windmill

where I live. It brings me back to my day in an essential way. When I do feel like taking a picture, I have an incredible amount of energy to spot nuance and beauty in ways that I find myself revisiting for weeks afterward.

When I take a picture, it forces an awareness of my surroundings. Instead of staring at my phone as I am walking down the street, focusing on texts or emails, I am looking at the seasons change, the flowers that are currently in bloom, the birds that are native to my region. There are things that I had never noticed before. I know so much more about the world around me than I ever did before. Beyond the local world around me, I feel more driven to travel and to create images from places that are more foreign to me.

This phenomenon of noticing has changed my relationship to my work, as all good art and self-care should. First, when my clients talk, I find that I am trying to picture their lives in more detail. I wonder what the bricks on their houses look like, the trees that they see when they walk home, the birds that chirp on their block. I wonder about sneakers hanging from the wires that are overhead. I wonder about the sunset by the train tracks, the colors of the graffiti on the concrete they pass by. Noticing more has made me want to notice everything. It has been a welcome, yet unintended, outcome of taking pictures.

This feels like the nuanced way that self-care should operate. It should accompany us throughout our days and be something that we can internalize and use to deepen our most mundane interactions. It should be something that we can integrate into our lives, rather than always removing us from our lives.

I don't know if I am a good photographer or not. I don't care. That is an incredible feeling for me. While I try hard to do excellent work daily, I embrace the mediocrity of my photography. Self-care should allow us to engage with parts of ourselves in an unpressured, unhurried, and non-competitive way. It should awaken the parts of us that don't need to succeed, but rather need to simply breathe and be.

I bought a camera, a real one. Then I signed up for a photography class. This kind of messed up the whole thing for me. I started to want to get good at it and make the most of the money I had invested in both. It took me a while to get back to just taking pictures for fun. I say this because I think that finding self-care that sincerely nurtures is a delicate and idiosyncratic process. It doesn't look the same for any two people, and it shouldn't. For me, taking care of myself requires a tender and delicate balance. It took some time to strike it. That's okay.

Real self-care, real art, is always a work in imperfect progress. Just like we are.

35. Self-Care, Clients as Tenants, and Peer Support

The issue of achieving "good" self-care at any time during one's social work career is a near universal one. First, what "good" self-care means varies from social worker to social worker. Some social workers need to have exercise in place to clear their heads. Others need excellent group supervision. Let me try to discuss, though, why self-care itself feels like such a complicated issue. Let me also attempt to address part of why there is something about the dialogue about self-care that can feel so frustrating and odd.

Simply put, the work we do is exceptionally hard. Yes, there are a lot of professions that do very complicated and difficult work. I am not arguing that. I am arguing that social work is uniquely complex for the psyche to metabolize. The fact is that when we are performing our job really well, we will see our clients walk out feeling tremendous relief. It is hard to say exactly why this relief is happening. There are a million reasons, and the reason is likely different every time. But there is likely a unifying reason why this relief is taking place, and that is because something transactional has occurred in the dyad between the client and the clinician.

Our clients are with us.

We ask our clients to rest their minds at our doorsteps. Many times, what we are also asking our clients to do is to part with significant pieces of their stress, to make them freer to function. But this stress, on a psychic level, has to go somewhere. I would argue that it floats into our minds, and it rents out space in the crevices and vacancies of our buildings. I think that as a social worker, it is fair to think of yourself as a building manager, with many different units, large and small. Clients come in and they make deposits in our minds—in our buildings—and we accept this. The clients don't stay forever, and we never know exactly how long they will stay, but we do hold things for them.

This is why, sometimes, we are in the shower and it feels as if we have a sudden realization about a client. We might be doing the dishes and the same thing will happen. We have our clients with us in ways that can feel both intimate and haunting. We have clients with us in ways that we can often feel ashamed about. This is because there is a lot of dialogue out there about boundaries and the need to have them. In fact, we need to have good ones. That is true. But this dialogue often produces an internal sense of shame or a punitive feeling driven by an overly regulated super ego that keeps us from sharing just how truly "with" us our clients are.

I want to echo that Carl Jung spoke eloquently about a collective unconscious and a psychological field that we coexist in with our clients. This field does not end when our work day ends. This fact does not dismantle, whether or not boundaries are present. But somehow, there is some confusion about all of this, and many new social workers are made to feel that if they take their work home with them, they have failed at creating good boundaries.

> No one has the self-care "thing" down. It is an elusive entity at best, so have patience for its unfolding and mysterious role in your life.

My hope is that self-care begins with separating these two dialogues. There is an important dialogue to be had about boundaries. There is another important dialogue to be had about how intense our treatment relationships feel and that we often wake and sleep with this, which does not render us unprofessional, naïve, or ill-prepared for this work. Self-care, in my opinion, begins with a level of acceptance about how deeply penetrating this work can feel, coupled with a surrendering of shame around that reality. We often conceive of self-care as a highly behavioral intervention, and it can be. It is also a mindset that allows us to recognize the gravity of our work, the extent to which it is not fully understood by other fields, and the very dangerous way that we, as social workers, can inappropriately police each other's boundaries in a way that silences our very real experiences of having our clients as tenants.

Peer support for self-care

My best advice, when it comes to self-care, if I have any advice at all, is that you need to hang out with other social workers. This does not need to happen all the time, but I do think it needs to happen. I think it can and should happen inexpensively. I think it is important to find a community of peers with whom you can talk about all of this shamelessly, honestly, and where the complexity of your role is celebrated and recognized.

I do not believe that this is something that can easily happen with co-workers. Relationships among co-workers in agencies and nonprofit settings are notoriously complicated. Yes, there is certainly support to be had, and it happens all the time. The cultivation of relationships outside of the agency setting can be a sincerely saving grace, free of the daily politics that dominate your workplace. It will allow you to have a place where you get to say what you need to say freely.

Beyond hanging out with other social workers, it is of particular import, in our field, to do things that give you renewal. This sounds trite, because it has been said a million times. It can mean journaling, art, or exercise. The bottom line, though, is that if you can't do those things for whatever reason, you need to pay close attention to protecting yourself from the shame that might ensue as a result. There is a very strong relationship between self-care and shame, and this is something that I hope you can find yourself feeling particularly on guard against.

No one has the self-care "thing" down. It is an elusive entity at best, so have patience for its unfolding and mysterious role in your life.

(Note: This meditation was originally published in my previous book, *Real World Clinical Social Work: Find Your Voice and Find Your Way.*)

PART 7

What To Do and How To Do It: The World of Assessment and Intervention

Rain

It is nearly impossible to photograph rain. It just moves too quickly and can't quite be captured. To see it clearly, one needs to step inside for a proper assessment. From within the safety of a windowed room, the beauty of rain becomes clear. And it is only from this windowed space that details of rain can be studied and communicated.

36. Alphabet Soup: EMDR, DBT, CBT, TF-CBT, IEP, ABFT, MBSR, MSFT, DSM, BPD, EBP, MSW

Eye movement desensitization and reprocessing therapy, dialectical behavior therapy, cognitive behavioral therapy, trauma focused cognitive behavioral therapy, individual education plan, attachment based family therapy, mindfulness based stress reduction, multi systems family therapy, diagnostic and statistical manual, borderline personality disorder, evidence based practice, and you—the MSW.

I started to think about all of the initials that we have to identify the treatments and interventions that we are supposed to use. Of course, we all know that we should be doing some sort of EBP. It used to be that the "most" evidence based practice was CBT, but now we have TF-CBT, which is great for kids, but if you have someone with BPD, you should use DBT, because that is more of an EBP. If you are working with families, MST used to be in vogue. Now there is focus on ABFT with a touch of MBSR. But you must really consult the DSM to decide how to best proceed with an IEP.

I am not saying any of this in jest, but it can start to feel quite silly. It can feel both quite complicated and reductive at the same time. It can feel confusing, because the pressure to produce "measurable" results from these interventions keeps growing alongside the pressure to adhere to a specific modality or theoretical orientation. I think it can leave us, often, wondering what we are doing at all and if we are doing it "right." In fact, the more prescriptive the intervention, the more likely we are to feel as if we are going off script and thereby getting it all "wrong."

So, what are we doing? I think that the answer, of course, varies from client to client and clinician to clinician. However, there are some powerful and unifying themes that I think we ought to be adhering to and, really, refusing to get distracted from. There are three central things that I am working on doing at all times, though it might not always seem obvious. These things are: *increasing emotional literacy, offering containment,* and *shifting toward a secure attachment style.*

Emotional literacy

Tremendous relief often comes for people when they recognize that they are having feelings, for these feelings to be named, and for the feelings to be witnessed and truly experienced. It can be surprisingly difficult to even identity the presence of a feeling for several intricate and subtle reasons. First, a feeling can only be understood if it was originally mirrored by a caregiver. For example, a kid could fall and cry. The caregiver could say, "It doesn't hurt, come on, just get up." Or a caregiver could say, "Oh, that must have been scary and really hurt." The responses lay the groundwork for future attempts to understand our own internal, emotional worlds. Secondly, defenses often obscure our access to emotions because something in us is saying that the emotion will be too scary to experience. Or we fear that the emotion might even annihilate us in some way. This is why some might opt for denial, dissociation. or intellectualization. It is not necessarily a conscious choice, but it is one that severs us from the deep knowing that comes from saying and facing our emotions.

So many of our interventions can be distilled down to the simple question: "How does that make you feel?" We return to this question in the hopes of enhancing emotional literacy, increasing the awareness of the geography of one's own mind. This deepened awareness leads to a freedom and a mastery. It is initiated by the curiosity of an other (us), and transformed into empowerment and self-knowledge for our clients.

Containment

Another central task in our clinical work is to offer containment. We have clients who come in worried, afraid, anxious, and even disorganized in their understanding of who they are. We have clients who have a terrifically hard time integrating varying pieces of themselves and their experiences into their psyches. Their time with us serves as a resting place for their psychic trouble. We offer the time, the space, and the steadiness to receive our clients fully.

For example, if a client has just experienced a surprising loss of a loved one, that client's brain has not yet accommodated to this reality. They wake up surprised about it having happened, and when they remember the loss, it can feel like a sudden jolt. Even if there are just minutes between the remembrance, that jolt is there. Clinically, we serve to contain them. We hold the information that the loss indeed occurred, that they will survive, and that their mind will eventually habituate to it. It is our keen awareness of their ultimate survival, coupled with our presence, curiosity, and tenderness, that allows for the evolution of their own ability to contain the pain and vicissitudes of their own mind.

Secure attachment

Moving someone from an anxious or avoidant style of attachment is not particularly complicated, though it is not easy. It requires a steadfast commitment to predictability, transparency, and adherence to the frame that is provided by our work. If we are prescribed a 45-minute hour by our agency and this is what we consistently work with, this helps to shift attachment. If we demonstrate that we remember what our client talked about last week, this shifts attachment. If we don't overwhelm with our presence, but don't disappear either, this shifts attachment. The more assuredly that we demonstrate that we have internalized our clients and their stories, and the more consistently that we show up, the more powerfully we can have an impact and shift their expectations about how attachment ought to go.

The alphabet soup matters. A lot of wisdom and research have gone into the discovery of different ways of practicing, thinking, and being. But don't let it divert you from the complexity of the basics, and the simplicity required to sustain and build human connection.

37. Questions That Deepen

Sometimes when I am sitting with clients, I picture where in their brains I can land a question. I know that sounds strange, but it's true. There are questions, mostly related to cognition, that keep clients located in their frontal lobe. There are also questions, most related to affect, that move clients more deeply into the hypothalamus (the location for flight or fight tendencies) or into their bodies. It isn't exactly that I privilege one location over another. Instead, it is that it is worth understanding the neurobiological AND interpersonal impact of the questions that we craft.

As clinical social workers, our most frequent go-to intervention is to ask questions. We can talk about validation, normalization, reflective listening, and the tendency to use these techniques, but the fact is that most of what we say takes the form of inquiry. It is an awesome reality that we have a shared interest in demonstrating authentic curiosity about our clients' lives. On the other hand, it is striking that we don't talk more about how to craft questions and the significance of the process of seeking more information from our clients.

Thinking about questions as tools that have an impact on the pacing of a session and that deepen self-exploration informs the crafting of what we see. The first thing that I consider when I ask a question is whether or not I am seeking to down- or up-regulate a client. What I mean by this is that there are times in a meeting or session when a client can seem particularly deadened or disengaged. It is at moments like this that I will create a question that ideally will up-regulate the client, or bring the client into the room, back to life. For example, simply asking, "What are you feeling in this exact second?" can accomplish this. You can also say, "Can you tell me where you are right now?" Notice, of course, the words "can you." The reason why I pad the question like that is that it gives the client a protective barrier between them, me, and the intensity of the question. I am not directly saying: "Tell me where you are right now." There is a way in which that can be experienced as intrusive and aggressive. In the work of up-regulating, it is often quite hard to also remain respectful of boundaries and sensitive psychological processes. But it can be done.

To down-regulate, to calm a client, I will often ask questions that might move them away from overwhelming affect. Although overwhelming affect is often a gift and essential to a client's work, it does not often help for a client to feel completely awash in intense emotion as a session nears the end. It is our responsibility, in many ways, to prepare our clients for re-entry into the world following the intimacy of our exchanges. These questions, for me, include, "What do you plan on doing after this?" or simply, "What are you thinking about as we wrap up?" The reason I would use the word "thinking" is that cognition can often stabilize someone's emotional state. If you move someone into the frontal lobe, with a question more directed toward that part of the brain, the hypothalamus can calm and soothe itself.

Beyond up- and down-regulation, I am also hoping to help clients begin to integrate their cognitions, behaviors, and affect states. There are several clinical interventions that seek to divide cognition from affect, but I am more interested in the integration of these parts of one's self. Psychological relief often comes from feeling what you are thinking and thinking what you are feeling. Let's say that a client is ambivalent about returning to their family of origin for the holidays. They might think that they are lazy and tired and don't feel like driving. They might feel terrified. The goal is to have them understand that they are not lazy, but in fact feeling something real, and if their thoughts can reflect that, more sound and relieving decisions can be made. But it is not just sound decision-making—having thoughts and feelings align enhances someone's sense of self and capacity for introspection. There are questions that make this possible, and they are usually informed by clinical observations of incongruencies. For example, an observation can be made and turned into a question: "You are saying you are lazy, but you also seem quite sad. I wonder what you make of that?" That question seeks to help clients better articulate their cognition. You could also say, "What do you make of the fact that you are feeling so sad, but your thoughts don't help us to better understand the sadness?"

Superficially straightforward, asking questions that shift, deepen, and create openings is a task that requires premeditation and savvy. We are often told not to ask our clients "why." I am not totally sure of where this idea comes from, but I do know that even the question, "Why?"—when well timed and intentional—can bring our work to life. Thinking carefully and feeling our way into the simple efficacy of the intervention of inquiry and curiosity is clinical social work at its best.

38. Assessing Through a Kaleidoscope: Part 1

I often marvel at the gap between what an intake form asks us to discover about a client and what it is that we need to know. Although there isn't a standard intake form, agencies strive to collect some similar information. The questions typically include a study of the history of the presenting problem, current stressors, drug and alcohol history, trauma history, financial stressors, perhaps some family and relationship history, maybe legal issues, and a sense of overall social functioning. These topics are of terrific import, but I am not sure that they support the depth of the relationships and conversations that social workers ought to be constructing.

I am not encouraging everyone to suddenly go off script. I do want to think about what pieces of information might serve to create an in-depth assessment, thereby creating more highly attuned interventions, clinical relationships, and treatment.

Let's start by talking about why a social work assessment is different from any other—or at least why it should be. The founding principles of social work are that we treat the whole person; that we see the person as a central part of the environment and the environment as a central part of the person; that we take race and socioeconomics intensely seriously; and that we pay vigilant attention to development, attachment, and trauma. For us to attend to these principles, we need to create a way of thinking about and performing assessment that honors them.

Further, when assessment is done well, it is a performance of true curiosity. We demonstrate to our clients that we are deeply interested in who they are and want to know about the major events in their lives as much as we want to know about the nuanced texture of their daily functioning. Curiosity, unto itself, is curative. We often forget that assessment is an intervention on its own, if it is done well. Just think about how it feels when someone asks you how you are doing, how your family is doing, and what you are stressed out about. The questions make you feel held and seen. The questions make you feel like you matter. Assessment, when done well, is an intervention.

How can we make it a truly powerful intervention? When I meet with someone, I have a lot that I want to know. In fact, I truly let my curiosity take over. If I am to sincerely surrender to my curiosity, rather than some pressure to assess "right," I find that my ability to assess is strengthened. When I don't rush through an assessment or think about what is on an intake form, I also find that my assessment is strengthened.

Here are some areas of true curiosity for me that I think echo our field's founding principles.

Past experiences with social workers

For any good assessment to take place, we need to get a good handle on the potential transference themes that might come up. We often think of transference as the placement of past familial dynamics onto clinical dynamics. That is certainly a central part of it. However, transference can also take a simpler form. Clients who have had negative experiences with social workers will be less open to new experiences with social workers. Clients who have only worked with interns will be less likely to confidently attach if their intern left in the middle of a good treatment alliance. We need to understand a client's attachment history to our field to get a sense of how they might be internalizing and preparing for their work with us.

We need to ask about it.

Birth story

I am almost always interested in someone's birth story. A birth story is a narrative told between generations. We rarely know if the information in a birth story is true or false, but we must pay real tribute to the power of the narrative. I have clients who don't know their birth stories. That is powerful information. I have clients who have birth stories that literally make no sense. That is powerful information. I have clients who say that their mother almost died during labor. That is powerful information. I also have clients who say that they almost died in birth. That is powerful information. There is no piece of information in a birth story that is irrelevant. It can almost all be considered symbolic and representative of larger life themes. If someone doesn't know anything about their birth, that means a lot about their access to information about their past. Perhaps they were adopted. Perhaps their mother was not conscious. Perhaps they are the youngest of 12 kids. No matter what, the data in a birth story are worthy clinical content.

We need to ask about it.

The history of their name

Every client's name has meaning. Perhaps they were named after their mother's favorite soap opera character (this happens a lot), or perhaps they were named after their great grandmother who died in the Holocaust. Held in a name is a story about how someone's life was imagined from the minute they were born. Perhaps there was a hope that they would fill a hole left by someone who died suddenly. Perhaps there was a hope that they would become the next president. I had an African American client who was named something that many White children are named. Her parents called it a "résumé name." I have another client who was named after her mother's best friend who had died in a car accident. Her mother always hoped that she and her daughter would be best friends. She hoped that they would spend many days doing activities similar to what she had done with her friend. When her daughter didn't have this interest, her mother's disappointment was complicated by grief. There is a story in every name. With every story, our assessment grows deeper.

We need to ask about it.

Attachment patterns

I always ask about a client's perception of their family's attachment patterns. Was there affection in their house? How often do they check in by phone? How old were they when they were first left alone? What does 7 p.m. in your home look like? Is everyone together on a couch watching TV? Is everyone in separate rooms? Did you eat dinner together? Are some people hungry while others are full? Was there enough food for the night? All of these questions bring you more closely into someone's reality. In doing that, we have a better sense of how their family attached to each other. Attachment patterns are almost always intergenerational, unless they are shifted by some confounding, healing, or hurting variable. For example, someone could have grown up in an extremely avoidantly attached family but went to a very loving school. Another could have grown up in a very securely attached family but suffered tremendous trauma. No matter what, patterns and disruptions in attachment are worthy of examination in assessing a client.

We need to ask about it.

Gender and sexuality

Issues of gender and sexuality are never simple. If you have a trans client who once identified as gay and now identifies as straight, there is a tremendous amount of data to collect around the client's internal experience of this. If you have a cis-gendered straight client, there is tremendous information to be collected about that experience, too. No one has a simple experience of their gender or their sexuality. I am cis-gendered, and I know that performing femininity feels complicated to me. I have many trans clients for whom the case is the same. I urge you to consider that *everyone* is having an experience of their gender and sexuality that is worthy of bringing into the clinical relationship. I also urge you to recognize the interconnected relationship between gender and sexuality. For those who don't feel comfortably seated within their gender, sexuality becomes much more complicated. For those who don't feel comfortably seated within their sexuality, gender becomes much more complicated.

We need to ask about it.

The bank account/The absence of the bank account

Every client, every client, *every* client, has a complicated relationship with money. We are often told (outside of the field) to never talk about money. Of course, the top three stressors in most conversations are traditionally considered to be: politics, religion, and money. We cannot let this sense of taboo keep us from allowing our clients to share their money stories. Perhaps we have clients who feel overwhelmed and ashamed by their privilege. This is information that might literally never be discussed if we don't inquire about it. More commonly, of course, we have clients who feel overwhelmed and ashamed by their poverty and struggle. They would never even want us to know about the depth of their shame and fear.

Think about how you feel when your cell phone rings and it is an 800 number that you have come to recognize as one of your many, confusing student loan lenders. You hit ignore, have a rush of adrenaline, and move on with your day until they call again tomorrow and you do it all over again. Many of our clients get these calls 20-30 times a day, if they can even keep a phone number over time. Many can't do that. This is information we need to have to understand the utter complexity of their daily stress and anxiety. We can't just say that they should think differently about their anxiety and pathologize their symptomology without having a behind-the-scenes view of how desperate their moment-by-moment financial struggle is.

We need to ask about it.

39. Assessing Through a Kaleidoscope: Part 2

Assessment needs to be an integral and ongoing piece of the overall treatment process. Thinking of assessment as dichotomously distinct from treatment relegates our period of inquiry to early sessions. It also leaves us hastily conclusive. Of course, the pressure to assess early is to produce a diagnosis for a client. These diagnoses are often used for immediate billing and to create a shared language within an agency about a client. For example, if we label a client as having schizoaffective disorder, then we can all agree about some of the primary traits of that client. Supposedly.

Before delving deeper into what can strengthen the assessment process, I think it is worth reflecting on the insanity of the pressure to be expected to come up with a diagnosis based on 45-50 minutes with someone. Sure, some intakes last longer—but certainly not long enough to label long-standing patterns of behavior, coping mechanisms, and defensive functioning.

Given that this expectation makes no sense in our effort to understand complex human functioning, it is fair to internally reconstruct our assessment process and to go with what feels most ethically right and dignified. I know that a lot of what I write about defies agency culture and expectations. My hope is not to describe anything that feels impossible or undoable for social workers. Instead, I am hoping that you find ways of interacting and assessing your clients that are more suited to *your* internal values than to agency standards. Dealing with the ensuing discrepancy that will come from this demands hard work and utter creativity.

That said, the more that assessment and intervention can be integrated, the more likely we are to create a well attuned intervention strategy that is based on our clients' unfolding life stories. To work with real people, we need to be flexible in our perceptions and in our treatment strategies. The best way to do this is to constantly check in with a client about how the assessment process is going. Perhaps they have an idea about what would help more. I think we often forget that our best supervisors are our clients. The more information we seek from our clients, the more effectively we can treat them.

Holding firm to the idea that one of our central assessment tools must be our authentic curiosity, here are some other areas that I try to learn more about when working on creating a treatment relationship.

What is your relationship with food like?

We often only think to inquire about someone's relationship with food when they are presenting with a traditionally identified eating disorder. In doing this, we miss a tremendous amount of information about non-diagnosable food relationships. Everyone has a relationship with food. There is no exception to that rule. Some people have a more complex relationship with food than others do. We often have the assumption that cis-gendered women struggle with food more than cis-gendered men. This negates a lot of truth about the male struggle with food. It also negates the unique struggle with food that exists for trans folks.

We often think that food struggles are limited to more privileged populations. This is also a dangerous misperception. Many food issues are born out of food insecurity and fears around scarcity. We need to give space for clients who felt that they had too much food. We also need to give space to clients who feel that they never had enough. We need to hold onto the real truth that food often acts as a metaphor in the psyche of clients. In the food relationship, we can identify feelings about being "too much," "never enough," and fears about insatiability and desire. Food themes are often life themes. And the discovery of life themes is far more important than any diagnosis.

What is your relationship with alcohol and/or drugs like?

Similar to food, we often assess for drug and alcohol issues when there is a stated problem. Most people, again, have some sort of a relationship with drugs and alcohol that holds important clinical data. Our questions ought not be limited to an excess use of substances. Instead, we can open a dialogue about the role that substances play in the home, in one's sex life, socially, and financially. We should also dedicate curiosity to the role of substances in one's family. If someone has had a loss that was due to overdose, their drug use holds specific meaning. I am eager to widen the conversation about substance use away from simply assessing for abuse. Instead, let's consider discussing the meaningful role that substances play in many lives.

Describe your block to me.

If we can't picture the home that someone returns to daily, we are missing something. As social workers, we are intensely interested in environment and the ways in which environment affects the psyche, although we are often remiss in our efforts to truly understand the texture of one's individual environment. If someone lives in a row home, I am curious about the neighbors. Do they talk to them? Do they live amongst family? Is the house next to them abandoned? If someone lives in a homeless shelter, I am interested in how the bed feels, how safe their belongings are, how many people are all falling asleep in the same room. If someone is in a neighborhood that they have been in for generations and it is becoming gentrified, I am interested in the presence or absence of grief around that. Is there a neighborhood grocery store? Do they hear gunshots at night? Is the walk to school safe? The list goes on. The central point is to learn enough to get a visual representation of one's neighborhood, so we can better understand the underlying stressors of one's daily life and we deepen our attempt to witness them.

How do you feel about your educational history?

There are feelings of pride, shame, disgust, terror, sadness, and triumph tied to educational experience. Some clients have graduated from Harvard Law School and still don't feel a sense of accomplishment. Other clients have not completed high school and are constantly hiding something about their sense of their own intellect. Many people have had great educations and are now drowning in student loan debt. Some people are continuing a family tradition of education, and others are terrified as they break the mold. Education in our country is a commodity and a piece of social capital. There is a lot of identity tied up in education that we often forget to talk about, because it is not a traditional area of clinical inquiry. In my experience, the study of one's educational history leads us to understand the person's psychological experience of this history.

How would you describe your family of origin's parenting style?

First, it is important to note that not all our clients have had parents in their lives. I think it is worth asking someone about who they identify as their family members. These can be friends, foster parents, or grandparents. We cannot assume the presence of a traditional nuclear family structure. However, whoever raised someone had a style of parenting or caretaking. The traditional styles are authoritarian, authoritative, and permissive.

I am not talking about that. Instead, I want to know if a family was boundaried, close, distant, enmeshed, chaotic, stable, rigidly married to routine, able to talk about difficult topics, overstimulatingly open, or parentifying. The list goes on. I am even curious about whether or not there were locks on the bathroom doors and if these locks were used. I am not interested in judging the answer—just making sense of it. Although it may seem like an inane level of detail, all of this matters. It matters because this information provides us with clues to the endlessly intricate puzzle of one's mind.

How would you describe your relationship with your body?

While the food topic might seem to cover the issue of one's body, it certainly does not. Of course, all our clients have bodies. Part of where treatment falls short is in the misconception that we are healing minds, which are somehow separate from bodies. Working from a holistic, social work perspective, we must endlessly respect the interplay between one's mind and body. There is, in fact, no real difference between the two. Some people feel strong in their bodies, while others are sure that their bodies will betray them by illness or injury. Some people feel completely imprisoned by their bodies because of past abuse and the resulting symptoms.

I like to ask people about their relationship with their bodies. I am always curious about the answer. Even in asking the question, we acknowledge—amelioratively—the sheer presence and fact of one's body. We disabuse them of the notion that they are invisible to us. This can be difficult, because invisibility can sometimes feel better than visibility. This is worth talking about. This is essential clinical data. If our psyches become injured, the scars reside in the body. We honor this truth by acknowledging this truth.

Intergenerational patterns

Some of the most subtle and abstract patterns of functioning that people deal with are the byproduct of intergenerational patterns of trauma and functioning. It can be incredibly useful to ask about struggles of past generations that clients are still aware of. For example, having ancestors who were part of the Holocaust or slave trade can have a lingering impact on the psyche today. Another example is to think about the intergenerational impact of immigration. Perhaps someone's parents or grandparents never learned to speak English, and the client largely serves as a translator today. This is of terrific psychological impact and ought to be introduced into any therapeutic dialogue.

Cultural, ethnic, racial identity

Obviously, we as social workers are concerned and mindful of the impact of oppression and difference. While no one has achieved a level of expertise around how to discuss difference, that does not mean that we can leave it out of our clinical discourse. It is essential to ask about someone's sense of who they are. A client's external appearance might be aligned with their sense of self. However, the more invisible differences are the ones that need utterance in the presence of another. We know that identity plays a central role in how someone functions in the world. The question for us is: *how?* How does it feel to be biracial? How does it feel to be queer in a conservative community? How does it feel to be the only African American student in a class of White students? It is not just how someone identifies, it is about *how* that identity is experienced.

We need to ask.

Our questions need to be crafted in a way that doesn't feel intrusive, doesn't feel assumptive, and doesn't feel rote. This is actual artistry. In fact, one of our biggest tools is the art of asking questions—very good questions. It is ultimately our work to help clients give voice to their internal worlds. It is only with attuned, empathic curiosity about the minor and major details of someone's life that this voice can be heard.

Yes, Ship

There was something called Big Ships Week in Philadelphia in 2015. This picture offers multiple juxtapositions. There is the Ferris wheel (for pure pleasure) juxtaposed with the ship (for pure work) against the shifting backdrop of clouds, which shift the way that the man-made objects look depending on their varying position. The clouds reign supreme.

40. Nothing But the Truth

As social workers, we are trained in the art of understanding relativity. We honor the context of our clients' lives. In this process, we often step aside from assumptions or hard conclusions. We work diligently to avoid an overly knowing stance, often deferring to the expertise of our clients. This is part of what makes our work so powerfully healing. We craft interventions that lead our clients to their inner wisdom and instinct. However, there are times when we need to surrender this stance, completely, in exchange for a staunch and clear knowing. There are times when our clients need definitive truths reflected back to them. It is our work to identify when to stay quiet and when to speak up, when to tell a truth, and when to yell a truth.

We step away from the stance of relativity when our clients are in danger. This danger needs to be clearly stated. For example, let's consider a woman who is in an abusive relationship. It is important to continuously weigh the pros and cons of remaining in this relationship. We can work to strategize safe vs. more dangerous times to leave. And, yes, we need to work with clients to create a plan that makes leaving possible.

Oftentimes, though, what gets lost in the deliberation and meditation around the choice to leave is the precise articulation of the peril that our client is facing. We need to be able to tell clients that we think they are at risk for dying. We need to talk openly about danger, injury, and death. It is our responsibility to offer a clear and unyielding articulation of the fact that staying still will only increase the traumatic impact of the relationship.

It is true that we need to consider our clients' processes and bear witness to how their awareness unfolds. But this does not mean that we abandon the painful responsibility of mirroring the truth. We must speak, unrelentingly, to how high stakes and fatal domestic violence can be.

This truth telling is particularly relevant when working with clients who have experienced sexual violence. Perhaps the violence was clearly rape, but sexual violations are rarely that simply defined. Instead, sexual intrusions can be subtle, elusive, and difficult to verbalize. Clinically, we must offer our clients relief from the psychic ambiguity generated by sexual violence. A hallmark of sexual violence, of course, is the experience of doubting that it happened at all. Our recurring commitment to reflecting the fact of sexual violence, our refusal to doubt that it occurred, our willingness to use language to bring it into the open, is essential and ameliorative.

A client who is going in and out of serious drug addiction also deserves the utterance of certain truths. A trait of addictive behavior is frequently denial. When someone is struggling with addiction, the risk for death comes into consciousness in fleeting moments. Our work, in these dynamics, is to hold firmly onto what has been disavowed in the service of denial. The potential consequences of dabbling in a world of deadly drug use, drugs that can easily result in overdose, need to be expressed. We need to tell our clients that we fear for their lives, that we dread the potential of their deaths.

> It is okay to tell your clients that you are worried about them. Speak from your humanity to theirs and tell your clients what you see.

Working with children in abusive homes complicates this principle. In these cases, it can be of great clinical import to include child protective services to best protect the child's safety. This is hard to do when you feel a level of skepticism in the "system." At the same time, it is often the best option available. Children in abusive situations often have to return to that situation. Because of their need to adapt to their own lives and to sustain their attachments, there is a real struggle for them to know, claim, and own their abuse. It is considerably painful, in these cases, to negotiate the voicing of truth in these cases.

My belief is that if a child is being abused, this needs to be said aloud to the child. I hold firmly to this even if the child needs to remain in the home. I argue for this because we risk being another person in that child's life who challenges their awareness of reality. Kids know what is happening to them, but they need adults to offer verbalization of this knowing. If we don't crisply affirm the truth of their mistreatment, they will likely doubt it, internalize it, and long struggle for a sturdy relationship with their own perceptions.

Our work is so incredibly complicated. There is no end to this fact. We honor all different ways of being in the world, make use of harm reduction, refrain from judgment, occupy not-knowing stances, while building on the expertise of others. Conversely, we serve as reality testers, corroborating stories that haunt our clients with doubt and insecurity. We act as auxiliary egos, helping our clients to see straight when their vision is blurred by their life circumstances. In providing this clarity and vision, we give voice to unbearable truths when every client defense is begging us not to.

- Is my husband dangerous? Yes.
- Can I die from relapsing on heroin? Yes.
- Is it okay for me to be alone at home when I am 5 years old? No.

We straddle the need to remain in gray space while also screaming out what is clearly black, white, right, or wrong. While this tension can feel untenable to hold, our attachments to our clients make the necessary discernment possible. By feeling our attachments, we are guided toward what needs to be said and when to hold our tongue. We are trained to feel defended against our attachment to our clients. But the use of our attachment and the clear articulation of it can be the one thing that might save them.

It is okay to tell your clients that you are worried about them, that you would miss them, that you cannot imagine your life without them. Speak from your humanity to theirs and tell your clients what you see.

41. Obscured Paths Toward Wellness

I used to think that all my clients were going to end up in graduate school—not just college, but graduate school. Although this was clearly a narrow view of things, and a fairly narcissistic one, it was my way of thinking that anyone can do anything. Sure, I was aware of the idiosyncratic desires of each client, but this was my way of honoring infinite possibility and wellness for anyone. I have come to understand many things since this original naïveté. Some of these things have to do with the futility of graduate school, but more significantly, I have come to understand the substantial variations in the presentation of progress and wellness.

We have clients with all different levels of functionality, of course. Since my initial graduate school for all fantasy, I have learned how hard it is to recognize both a client's strengths and real suffering in equal measure. I have clients who have begged me for years to see how much pain they are in and how limited they feel in their functionality. I have also had clients who have asked me to understand the level of satisfaction that they feel in their lives, even if I can't understand where that satisfaction is coming from.

To work with clients, from both a strengths-based perspective and in a diagnostically and socioeconomically precise way, we must listen beyond what we have the capacity to hear. In a recent case conference, we reviewed a case of a client who has been talking for years about the possibility of his own space travel. He intends to spend some time on Mars and bring his discoveries back to earth. He has no money, is often hungry, and is in poor health. At 45, he also has no education. Clearly, his goals are unrealistic. So what? He comes to meet with his social worker weekly, but no progress seems to be made. He just talks and talks and talks. She is often bored and frustrated. Where will the wellness come, and what will it look like?

During a recent session, he was talking about his strong political leanings, assuming the therapist felt the same. She felt invisible and enraged. The following session, she returned to say that she didn't agree with all his viewpoints, but was always open to hearing what he had to say. She felt it was essential to assert the fact of her existence in his life, in his mind, in his presence. He didn't blink when she said it, and he returned to space travel. She was dispirited and disillusioned. The next session, he came back to say that he had thought about what she said and he was grateful that she had shared her point of view.

To me, this is a tiny act of growth and wellness. Or maybe not so tiny. The client, in his psychological machinations, was operating from a highly narcissistic place. His ideas for his future are grandiose, and his capacity for relatedness is deeply diminished by his fantasy life and his struggle with self esteem. After endless sessions of reflective listening, a quintessential intervention for many narcissists who are struggling to locate and refine their senses of self, he was able to recognize another—an other. For this client, the path toward wellness might be the simple experience of moments of relatedness. Not necessarily a life of relatedness, but moments of it.

For every client, clearly, treatment goals and paths toward wellness or relief look different. The loftier our clinical goals are, the more likely we are to miss essential strides toward change and maturation. Sometimes, it feels painful to recognize the limitations of how much someone can change. Other times, it is generous to do this, because it is a complete honoring of the gravity of their internal struggle. I don't think someone with an extreme eating disorder will ever eat with complete freedom. Does this mean that I am giving up on them? Or does this mean that I am seeing them clearly?

Perhaps as we practice, over time, we may feel more cynical. But, really, I think it is that we become generously attuned and realistic. And, in this realism, we also understand that diversity in functionality is diversity in wellness. The more that we surrender a homogenic vision of what functioning or normal looks like, the more open to the vicissitudes of it we can become. Further, distilling our perception of wellness to something simpler can enhance our work.

I have come to think of my hope for all clients, now, as the capacity to attach. It was once graduate school, a privileged and monolithic notion. It is now attachment of any kind—to a pet, a type of food, a home, a friend, a dream. I have come, now, to recognize that the pulse of change can be measured by the ability to connect. Measuring the often subtle, and barely audible, diverse ticking of this pulse is where my work now lies.

42. Tenderly Assessing Suicide

I don't think of myself as an expert in suicide assessment by any stretch of the imagination. However, I have come to cultivate some ideas about how to stay connected to clients who are in the throes of suicidality. It has taken some time to achieve any inner calm around suicidal clients, because working with suicidal ideation and/or intent is some of the scariest work that we do.

Staying open to clients who feel intense isolation because of their wish to die requires a steady openness to our own darkness. This openness often defies much of what feels clinically instinctual.

The primary means by which I find myself able to connect with suicidal clients is to reserve judgment about how they are feeling. We often feel so pressured to properly assess for suicide that we are placed in a heightened state of judgment, often removing us from the empathy that calming suicidality requires. When we are jerked into a suicide assessment by noticing at-risk client behaviors, we often abandon our clients in search for an answer: *Are they safe or are they not?*

If we can slow the urgency and anxiety that accompanies assessment, we can engage our clients with curiosity. The fact is that inside all of us is a place that deeply understands suicidality. Perhaps we have not considered suicide, but we still know it in some way. Almost every person can answer the question about how they would kill themselves. It is just something that we have almost universally considered. It is an upsetting thought, but a compelling one. The fact that we can end our own lives is one that is psychologically gripping, if not fascinating.

We also all have something that we live in horrible fear of (loss of a loved one, a job loss, illness) and have wondered what would happen if that thing happened. We have considered that we might kill ourselves if our fear came true. For the most part, we know that we wouldn't take that route, but the idea is certainly not completely foreign to us. There is some comfort in the possibility. It is a terrifying comfort, yet it stands there as a hypothetical, though improbable, option.

Our minds also play weird tricks on us. This is particularly true around issues of suicide and death. Sometimes if I walk past a knife and see my cat, I wonder what would happen if I stabbed my cat. I love my cats more than I can even say. I would never stab them. However, this curiosity and wonder moves through me. It has no power, no resonance. It just passes through. For people who are struggling with intense depressive states and suicidality, the fantasies don't just pass through. Instead, they get stuck on the thought and it can become almost metastatic in its ability to become an obsession.

If we are to open to our own knowing of the ways our minds work, the suicidal client becomes more knowable, accessible, and far less scary. If we can open to the parts of ourselves that know the suicidal client, we better accompany them on their journey. Further, we can perform an assessment that keeps us from othering our clients in a way that makes them feel more alone than they already do.

We know our suicidal clients. We know them if we let ourselves into the depths of our own psyches.

Part of my strategy in working with suicidal clients is to surrender to the need to bravely and unwaveringly discuss what is going on in the client's mind. There is a lot of debate about whether or not doing this gives more power or gravity to the suicidal wishes. From what I have witnessed, quite the opposite is true. The more a client can give voice to what is in their internal world, the more benign those thoughts and feelings can become. In a vacuum, the thoughts feel fatal. In the light of day, their power is lessened.

Our work when assessing suicide is incredibly nuanced and demanding. We need to delineate between suicidal thoughts, ideation, and intent. We need to determine the difference between self harming behaviors and suicidal behaviors. We also need to try to access parts of people's minds that are often siphoned off with a lock and key. It is only with an unabashed look inside of ourselves for the connective tissue to soothe the isolation of our clients that we can properly perform this complex assessment work. Further, with a strong willingness to hear what clients feel is unutterable, we can start to ease the unrelenting impact of the obsessive power of suicidal tendencies.

We don't often talk about the bravery that suicide assessment takes. It is gut wrenching and soul stirring work. Done well, we are drawn into conversations about the deep wish that many feel for the relief that death would supposedly bring. Placed squarely on the side of life and safety, we walk on a tight rope. We bear witness to the strong seductive current of the wish to die as we move toward inviting our clients back to shore, alongside our welcoming sands.

43. Rethinking Addiction Treatment

Even if you don't work in a specifically designated addiction treatment setting, as a social worker, you surely interface with addiction. Although we think of addiction as most commonly associated with substance or alcohol abuse, addiction is pervasive and comes in many forms. Some people are addicted to sex, gambling, or food. We are all addicted to our phones, social media, and the little tingle of a "like." The tendency to think of those who have addictions as distinct from "us" is one of the central ways in which we become detached from our clients. There are many other ways we remain detached from our most vulnerable, addicted clients, heavily worthy of reconsideration and reconceptualization.

While we are steadily dedicated to the destigmatization of mental illness, drug and alcohol addiction falls outside of our efforts. With no clear research or supporting evidence, our thinking about addiction is guided by forces that only lead to increased isolation of this treatment population. Living in America leads us to think about people who have addictions as individuals with moral failings that range from plain sin to full-on criminality. These individuals are often punished in their treatment settings or in jail. Either way, the biases that we hold against clients with addictions are not serving to improve the epidemic of substance abuse.

Myths about people with addictions

There are myths about people with addictions that seem to be widely shared.

- First, it is almost universally believed that they are manipulative and drug seeking. We believe that most operate in search of their next fix and have the capacity to do almost anything to accomplish this fix.

- Second, we subscribe to the notion that they are inherently amoral, selfish, and solely interested in caring for themselves.

- We also lean toward overestimating their capacity for destructive behavior, believing that they are capable of theft, abusive behavior toward others, or destruction of property.

- Perhaps most insidiously, we believe that many people who are addicted are making a choice to continue to act in ways that perpetuate their illness, not fully recognizing the powerful role that physiology plays in sustaining addiction.

Myths about addiction treatment

There are several myths that are almost unconsciously subscribed to in the treatment of clients with addictive disorders. These are the most pervasive.

- The only way that addicted people get better is through the provision of "tough love," which is typically enacted in the form of just plain toughness.

- Yelling at clients with addictions works.

- They need strict rules in their treatment to manage their inherently manipulative behavior.

- Most acts of generosity toward these individuals are enabling, and we, as treatment providers, are incredibly susceptible to enabling our clients.

- We are often blind to our clients' manipulative behaviors.

- A full blown intervention is typically required for someone to get serious about treatment.

- Drugs cannot help clients get off drugs.

- We can never see our clients when they are high; this gives them the wrong message.

- People with addictions cannot have loving relationships.

- The only real way for a client to ultimately get better is through embracing the 12 steps.

- Only those recovering from addictions can provide addiction treatment.

Possible points of reconsideration

What is so powerfully compelling about many of these myths is that, while we may subscribe to them, they feel counterintuitive. We often find ourselves following treatment guidelines that may feel cruel, withholding, or just plain uniform as opposed to appropriately idiosyncratic.

For the most part, people become addicted to self soothe. Whether the self-soothing is to manage physical pain—often originating from a prescription from an actual medical doctor to manage an early childhood trauma—addiction is born out of an inability to tolerate vulnerability, disappointment, or the sequelae of trauma. Many have unbearable internal worlds and will do what they can to flee their own psyches. Others have developed tremendous numbness and use substances to access their own psychic worlds. Often, addiction needs to be medically managed before being psychologically managed, to calm the body's intense physical suffering and withdrawal.

When physically balanced, through medicine, the psyche of the person with an addiction comes into view. This view allows us to see that they often have fragile egos that are only sent into deeper fragmentation when faced with tough love and treatment that withholds. Addicted people, although often appearing unboundaried, are simply trying to manage what feels internally chaotic. While boundaries are extremely important when working with them, it is not because the client will always take advantage of the clinician. Instead, it is because they are often of a psychological age that is far younger than their chronological age, and the provision of boundaries serves to contain and maturate the person who is addicted.

People who are addicted are also often incredibly loving and feel intense feelings of love for the people in their lives. The deeper issue is that they hate themselves and feel as if they ought to erase themselves, through substance abuse, to make the lives of their loved ones more manageable. While many of their behaviors seem selfish, in their minds, their choices often feel like the most generous option. Instead of crying to a mother or father, or asking for help from a sister or brother, they will turn their emotional needs inward—leaving them with demanding desperation that needs to be managed somehow.

Also important to note is that negative consequences do not have a particularly remarkable impact on the psyche of a person who has an addiction. Of course, if negative consequences worked, like the many that are disseminated in treatment settings, the clients would have stopped using quite a while ago. Instead, they feel subhuman, leaving them desperately dehydrated for self-respect. The provision of respect, tenderness, and warmth soothes many of the clinical needs of these clients.

Because so many people with addictions have had significant early attachment ruptures, our work needs to shift into the realm of tender, steady attachment. When we treat our clients punitively, which happens in many settings (i.e., withholding cigarettes, phone calls, social privileges), we activate their feelings of rejection. It is precisely these feelings of rejection that underlie most powerful triggers to use. Essentially, they live in unending double helixes of shame. When our treatment choices get hooked into these shame spirals, like staging interventions, asking clients to repetitively and publicly share their stories, we send our clients further down paths of panic and isolation.

Addiction work is truly trauma work. Trauma work requires deep attunement; recognition of developmental capacity and limitations; and steady, vigorous attention to the relationship— because ultimately, it is the internalization of relationships that finally offsets the need for the self-soothing that substances provide. Often, the only chance for this type of relationship occurs in treatment. We must capitalize on the potential of this corrective experience rather than subscribe to treatment doctrine that can be experienced as counterintuitive, counterproductive, and hurtful.

Abandoned

I had a student I loved named Scott. We connected one day when he wrote a paper about finding and nurturing his sobriety. I am sober, too, and we connected around this. Part of the way he keeps himself sober is with photography. His thrill seeking has shifted into art seeking. He took me to an abandoned building in Philadelphia to show me how the light penetrates the broken windows and the stunning graffiti that is illuminated by this light. This picture feels like an example of honoring the art of another by using my lens to broaden the exposure of their art and sharing my experience of it.

PART 8
Demystifying Dominant Tropes

Reflecting Trees

It is fascinating to see the way water reflects trees. I can't get enough of it. As if the awe-inspiring fact of trees is not enough, water goes to provide its own interpretation of it. And its interpretation is always filtered through the wind, which tells the water how to make the trees look.

44. The Myth of the Perfect Intervention

I want to address the powerful myth of the "perfect" intervention or the search to say the "perfect" thing. I often hear students and supervisees struggling to figure out what to say or what to "do" from one clinical moment to the next. I think that we are all haunted by the myth that the perfect clinical social worker (whoever that may be) would always know the perfect thing to say, and we can never match up to that person, that image. Our fantasies tell us that, perhaps, with enough training we might be able to figure out what the elusive thing is ourselves.

I had a client who recently disclosed a sexual assault that he had experienced when he was 15 years old. It wasn't that he didn't remember the assault; it was just that he wouldn't let himself understand it for what it was until recently. He knew that something inappropriate had happened, but felt ambivalent about allowing it to affect him in the ways that it very powerfully had. In many ways, accepting his assault meant a shift in his self perception. He needed to consider that he was a victim and survivor. Up until this point, he had understood himself to be just like everyone else, whatever that means.

My first fear when he was telling me was: *has he told me this before and I forgot it?* My second was: *how can I say the right thing? What is the right thing? I don't want to mess this up!* There are so many different routes to take, right? I could validate him and say, "You are incredibly brave for calling this what it was and owning it." I could practice reflective listening and say, "This sounds very hard." I could also employ some normalization and offer that "many survivors take time to understand what happened to them and let that in." I could also ask a series of open-ended questions, "Can you tell me more about what happened?"and "What feelings are you having around this experience?"

None of these options are wrong, are they? I don't think so. So if none of them are wrong, how can there be one that is precisely "right"? The fact is that there is no single right thing to say at any clinical moment. The other fact is that it is perfectly okay to get it wrong.

Because in clinical encounters, we have the chance for repair. What makes an intervention right, or good, or useful, is one that keeps the client talking. What makes an intervention right, or good, or useful, is one that keeps the relationship strong. Often, there is not even a word that needs to be said at all. Often, our silence is the most valuable instrument that we can offer.

Our work, really, is to keep our clients feeling safe with us, safe within their own minds, and safe to keep exploring what feels incredibly unsayable and unthinkable. My client, by even entertaining the devastating reality of his assault, was both remarkably brave and vulnerable. For me to flee into the interiors of my own mind, in search of the perfect thing to say and the perfect way to be, would be a defense on my part and an abandonment of him.

A lot of the thinking we do when we are in session is avoidance of the intimacy that is created by the spontaneity that is required of simply being with an other. A lot of the thinking that we do when we are in session also removes us from the essential idiosyncratic reality of each unique clinical dyad. So perhaps instead of searching for the perfect thing to say, we might benefit by surrendering to the impossibility of the search and realize how naturally the actual relationship guides us to say, simply, the next best thing.

45. The Impostor Phenomenon and the Social Worker

Whereas feelings of being a fraud or impostor are commonly associated with being a new social worker, these psychological states are endemic to clinical social work practice across all stages of experience. Some social workers talk openly about feeling like an impostor, while others keep their feelings private and to themselves. Regardless of how the experience is handled, it is difficult to negotiate and even harder to find our way out of it.

The term *impostor phenomenon* was originated by two clinical psychologists, Dr. Pauline R. Clance and Dr. Suzanne A. Imes (1978). The term was coined to capture the psychological fear of being found out, of walking around feeling as if one is faking it, or generally feeling as if one's own knowledge and skill are simply being performed, rather than authentically held and felt.

While Imes and Clance called this sensation "impostor phenomenon," D.W. Winnicott spoke about the concept of a true or false sense of self. He declared that developmentally, children sense what their caregivers most want and shape themselves according to these perceptions. Rather than evolving organically and authentically, children censor their emerging selves in the hopes of pleasing their caregivers and subsequently securing the attachment. It is argued that once a false sense of self is performed, accessing a truer sense of who we are becomes incredibly difficult.

Whether it is referred to as a feeling of fraudulence, impostor phenomenon, or a false sense of self, it is a psychological state that makes our work difficult, uncomfortable, and dissatisfying. In fact, estimates show that 40% feel this way, while other research has found that nearly 70% of all workers have had this feeling at one point in their professional lives. Perhaps the reasoning behind feelings of inauthenticity is inexplicable in social work, but I think there are some real reasons we are left feeling this way. Further, I think the illumination of these reasons might help liberate us from feeling like clinical impostors.

Theory

The fact is that most of us graduated from social work schools where the training was problematically generalist. The courses often end up feeling like survey courses. Each week is dedicated to a particular theory or intervention. For example, one week is spent on CBT, object relations, or motivational interviewing. We are assigned three articles or one book chapter, and the exploration of the topic is done. The discontinuity between topics from week to week makes it hard to internalize any one way of thinking.

We then enter work settings that claim to use one type of intervention or theory. For example, many settings that work with childhood abuse now almost exclusively use TF-CBT (trauma-focused cognitive behavioral therapy). Many substance abuse settings rely on motivational interviewing or the 12 steps. You probably didn't read much about these interventions in school, and you are left with a manual, and *perhaps* a few trainings and worksheets. Between you and a client, the fact is that you don't religiously use TF-CBT or any other theory, for that matter. We all practice, to some extent, eclectically. This is a byproduct of both our clients' needs and the nature of how we were taught in school—a little of this and a little of that. The mismatch between what is expected of us and what we are doing leaves us feeling as if we are faking it. We are not sure whether we are getting it wrong, but we know that we aren't doing as we are told.

> **Every time we sit with clients and bear witness to the complexity of their internal worlds, while seeking to make scarce resources go as far as we can, we are social work warriors, not impostors.**

Paperwork

The levels of paperwork we are required to do are invariably burdensome. The most problematic aspect of this is that paperwork almost always requires us to create some sort of fiction. More and more, paperwork asks for target treatment goals and progress notes that correspond with these treatment goals. Further, these treatment goals are supposed to be crafted in increasingly quantitative ways, counting the presence of symptoms, and—ideally—symptom reduction as the treatment weeks pass.

The expectations completely fly in the face of how humans function. Improvement cannot always be quantitatively measured, rarely happens in a linear fashion, and is nominally goal oriented. Progress is unpredictable, treatment goals are difficult to articulate, and symptoms are not experienced numerically. So, we are left to either treat our clients according to the demands of the paperwork, which leaves us feeling as if we are somehow abandoning them, or we treat our clients in a way that feels more authentic and end up falsifying or editorializing the work we did to best fit the note. Either way, we are left feeling less than honest and more than uneasy.

Supervision

The fact of the matter is that when we receive supervision in our workplaces, which many of us do, it is difficult to be honest with our supervisors. First, much of our supervision is spent reviewing tasks, paperwork, and adherence to agency standards and rules. Second, supervision often demands us to act as if we are much more loyal to the agency treatment modality than we usually are. Supervision often asks us to downplay the intimate realities of our treatment relationships, because discussing these truths leaves our supervisors fearing that we are unboundaried and unethical. We rarely discuss the ways in which we self-disclose in supervision, and we certainly stay away from talking openly about how strongly we feel about our clients.

Just like children who offer up a false self to maintain their attachment to their caregivers, we often offer up a false image of who we are professionally to keep the peace at our work, and to keep our jobs.

Impossible tasks

I truly believe that among the most powerful reasons that we are often left feeling fraudulent as social workers is the fact that we are asked to do too much with too little—acting as if we can pull off what is often impossible or untenable. For childcare workers, visiting a child's home one time to determine whether or not to open a case is not enough. But with 30 other cases, one visit must suffice much of the time. For medical social workers, discharge planning is typically something to satisfy the standards for discharge paperwork, but rarely represents the reality of what patients need when they leave a hospital. For inpatient mental health settings, with acutely suicidal clients, we must act as if the three to five days of treatment (allowed by insurance) will be adequate for someone to be re-set and committed to life.

We are, often, asked to fake. We are then surprised by the many ways in which we feel fraudulent, keeping these shameful feelings to ourselves.

Don't hide

What I know, with a decent amount of certainty, is that feeling like an impostor takes a toll. What I also know is that many of us are doing even more than our best, rendering us anything but fraudulent. Our sound intentions, attunement to our clients' idiosyncratic needs, endless flexibility, and creativity all render us highly authentic. Even when we do our work drained and depleted, we are truly trying to straddle multiple systems while remaining engaged with clients who desperately need us.

Perhaps rather than continuing to internalize feelings of falseness, we can begin to articulate the multiple external factors that conspire to make us feel "less than." In recognizing and naming these forces, a truer sense of self can evolve. Because the truth is that every time we sit with clients and bear witness to the complexity of their internal worlds, while seeking to make scarce resources go as far as we can, we are social work warriors, not impostors.

46. On Grief and Its Permutations

There is so much that we get wrong about grief, and it isn't surprising. Like most things in life, we are desperately trying to keep an unwieldy process orderly and comprehensible. The fact about grief, though, is that it is neither. Grief, by its very nature, defies simple understanding. Despite our efforts to stage grief or to divide types of grief into distinct categories, the unpredictability and idiosyncrasy of each grieving process sustain.

In our clinical work, a more nuanced understanding of grief can only serve to enhance our efforts with clients. It is first essential to note that grief is neither trauma nor depression. The difference between these words is not mere semantics. Instead, these are highly distinct phenomena. *Trauma* is the byproduct of an unpredictable and nonsensical attack on our attachment world. We can lose someone to a car accident or something else sudden; this does not automatically mean that we will become traumatized. That is because death is part of life, and despite its unpredictability, our minds are essentially designed to metabolize loss. Further, while grief often looks like depression, the underpinnings of each are quite distinct. *Depression* is a process by which our minds suspend our ability to motivate and function. *Grief,* while appearing to lack motivational properties, is us moving through something in a way that is often disruptive, but subtly productive as well.

There is really nothing unhealthy about grief. Grieving is something that our brains have been wired to do. It can make us feel as if we are going crazy, but it is actually our effort to grapple with experiences that feel nearly incomprehensible. We start to run into trouble with grief when thoughts about how grief *should* be inhibit the nuances of our individual processes. Here are some basic guidelines that might aid you in working with your clients around grief.

There is no timeline; there are no stages.

Grief often does not start immediately after a loss and can actually show up any time. Clients often feel that their grieving process ought to be limited to the societally allotted amount of time given. This is traditionally understood to be about a year. The fact is that grief can last weeks or decades. Also, grief never really ends. We might experience times when we are more in the heightened throws of it than other times, but it rests in us and can become unpredictably reawakened. For example, if we lost a mother at some point and feel that we have worked through this, the feelings are almost invariably reawakened when we become parents. The grief lies dormant and can reemerge, and this is normal.

We grieve far more than death.

Grief is not limited to losing something or someone to death. While grief is most commonly associated with losing a loved one to death, the fact is that grief insidiously affects many different life processes. In fact, the loss of a home to moving, graduation, or simple life shifts can be one of the most stirring forms of grief. The loss of a job is also quite grief-inducing. Any process that signifies the passage of time, a process that we lack complete control over, can elicit feelings of grief.

Intimacy and depth of grief are not positively correlated.

The level of closeness that we had to someone has no predictable bearing on the level of grief that we experience. There are times when we lose someone we were incredibly close to and the grief feels manageable. There are also times when we lose someone who was quite distant to us, perhaps a childhood teacher or a distant neighbor, and we find the grief difficult to regulate. This is often because society does not have ways in which untraditional grief is recognized and held. We are allowed to cry and miss work over losing a family member, but rarely for a crossing guard or any other figure in our life that represented stability and calm. The fact that society has a narrow tolerance for the types of grief that we are allowed to feel limits our ability to emotionally explore the depths of our own processes.

We talk to the dead.

Many of us talk to the dead. This is not something we are actually allowed to talk about unless it is cloaked in a religious tradition, but the fact remains that most of us walk around engaging in conversations with both the living and the dead, and this is completely understandable. Conversations don't just end because life does. Our clinical work is to bring our clients' relationships with those they have lost into sessions. We need to normalize the process of communicating with the dead and acknowledge the health of the effort to remain connected to those we have loved.

Not all grief has to become goodness.

There is nothing someone needs to do about the fact that they have lost someone. There are innumerable ways to honor the dead or the lost, such as 5k races or lighting candles or speaking out. However, the need to do something "good" to manage feelings that are experienced as "bad" is simply not psychologically necessary. It can be completely healing for some, but the meaning-making process of loss is one that does not need to be demonstrated altruistically or publicly.

Complicated grief

While grief can become trauma because there is no outlet for it or the loss was so shocking that the brain cannot accommodate it, the more likely scenario is that *typical* grief has become complicated grief. *Complicated grief* is actually what occurs when we are not able to tell the whole truth about the person or experience that we lost. For example, let's say that a client had a largely complicated relationship with their father. Everyone considered the father to be a hero, but privately this is not the client's experience. Or, someone feels shame around a loss, such as when they lose someone to a drug overdose. When someone needs to perform something inauthentic about grief, this can manifest itself in a complicated grief. A complicated grief is basically an inability to have a life that exists beyond the grief and to allow one's identity to become fused with the grief. It can also be related to denial over the loss that persists over time and disallows someone from integrating other aspects of reality.

Grief is a part of life and a beautiful part, at that. It is not always sadness, but sometimes joy, too. It is unpredictable, but also essential. It is a part of the human existence that ultimately forces us to face our own mortality, giving more life force to our days and our loving, and texture to our psychic landscapes.

Bird of Grief

Just three days after a beloved family friend died, this city bird landed on my back. I was walking down a crowded street with my son when the bird chose me as her temporary home. I was stunned and sure it was my friend. I felt that she came to visit me, in her new form, to let me know that she would always be around me. I placed her gently on this planted tree, and she nestled right in. I stared at her foggy eyes and wondered if she could see, if she was old, if she would find her way home. More than anything, I loved her.

47. Saying No to Gratitude and Forgiveness

It is tempting to simply say, "bah humbug." I want to write about how difficult the holidays can be with the constant pressure to feel happiness and joy. But the truth is that everything about the holidays has already been written. There are books and articles about how to be happy and embrace joy. There are books and articles about how to be unhappy and to embrace pain. The fact is that there is very little about the holidays that is left unsaid. However, perhaps said a bit less frequently is something that truly irks me about the holidays. This is the oppressive pressure to dually feel both gratitude and forgiveness.

The insidious and universal buy-in about the sheer "goodness" of gratitude and forgiveness feels frighteningly unquestioned and reductive. The ideas of gratitude and forgiveness, although not necessarily intertwined, are often sold together as sister products that need to be fully purchased on the road to emotional freedom and health. This feels as true for us as it does for our clients, therefore separating the pressure we feel to forgive and feel grateful from what our clients feel is fruitless and falsely dichotomous.

Let's start with how gratitude and forgiveness are sold.

Gratitude, slightly more nouveau in its marketization, is the idea that if we are to be thankful for what we have, we will feel happier. If we are to recognize that fact of abundance in our life, then the nagging feelings of scarcity will fall away. If we don't have material abundance, we are to recognize our relational abundance. If we don't have relational abundance, we are to recognize our spiritual abundance. If we don't have an abundance of health, we must feel grateful for our beating heart. In fact, if you Google "gratitude," the first page that comes up is from *Psychology Today.* That speaks very powerfully to just how much we have started to think of gratitude as an intervention that leads to mental health and stability. There is really nothing that is free of gratitude these days. You can find soap, underwear, socks, candles, journals, episodes of Oprah, podcasts, coloring books, necklaces, and t-shirts with the word "gratitude." The list goes on.

The idea of *forgiveness,* of course, is not quite as well marketed or trendy. But it certainly has the same enduring staying power as gratitude. While the roots of gratitude are largely Buddhist, the roots of forgiveness are in Christianity and Jesus, who spoke of forgiveness when on the cross. He stated: *Father, forgive them, they do not know what they are doing.* This is such a lovely notion—the idea of making room for those who do not know the error of their ways, who live in ignorance and are immune to the knowledge of the destructive nature of their own power. Not all religions are equally subscribed to the idea of forgiveness, but it certainly does seem to have transcendent power in society. There is a largely shared belief that emotional and psychological freedom comes with forgiveness. This idea is espoused by everyone from Dr. Phil to Mother Theresa.

First, I want to be clear that I am not specifically criticizing either of these ideas. Instead, I want to call into question any idea that is subscribed to with near universality. The more unquestioned a psychological notion is, the more suspicious of it we ought to be. Our work as clinical social workers is to think critically in a completely unwavering manner. Therefore, if there are concepts as pervasively popular as these two, we need to wonder why. If there are ideas about what creates wellness that are lacking the idiosyncrasy necessary to treat individual clients with unique stories, attachment styles, and trauma histories, we need to wonder why.

While I think that there might be tremendous possibility for relief in the act of gratitude and the movement toward forgiveness, I also think that these two ideas can be conceptualized as forms of social control.

I was working with a client recently who disclosed a long history of incest by her brother. She started to consider the idea of not inviting him to her birthday party. The idea of excluding a sibling from a family tradition is a radical one that takes a lot of strength and resilience. When discussing this idea with a priest, she was given a 25-page pamphlet on the power of forgiveness. This document, like many, contained a good amount of information about how no one is free until they forgive. It also contained a lot of information about the toxicity of anger and how anger keeps us stuck.

I disagree.

I think that anger, in response to abuse and violation, is essential. I don't necessarily even think that anger is something that someone needs to move beyond, because it often keeps us safe and protected from relationships that can truly damage the sanctity of our own minds and bodies. Anger is a piece of hyper-vigilance. Hyper-vigilance is often a byproduct of trauma. This is our internal system on alert for danger. While hyper-vigilance is not an ideal state of affairs because of the neurobiological impact of sustained exposure to it, it also contains vital information. This information defies forgiveness and gratitude, and instead honors safety and self preservation.

The fact is that many of our clients don't have a lot to be grateful or forgiving for. During the holiday season, this feels more palpable and real than during the rest of the year. While consumerism is at its highest and the exclusive nature of family reigns supreme, the power of loss and grief is most bitingly felt. The stinging reality of what many *do not* have is impossible to ignore. To focus on gratitude during the holidays reeks of a certain internal and societal denial.

What if we started to really look at the food that we are fed? Metaphorically (and literally, too)? Would we realize that the ideas and psychological "nutrients" that are most profusely served are born out of larger efforts to create silence and complacency? No, it isn't this simple. Nothing is. But it is certainly worth considering the real work of tolerating suffering and scarcity, rather than acting as if the mind can simply move us beyond these essential states of truth.

PART 9
Clinical Social Justice,
We Were Made for This

Proper Graffiti

There is a spot in Philadelphia called Graffiti Pier. It is right on the water, and the depth of the graffiti goes on and on. One can think of Graffiti Pier as a sociological or anthropological study of how Philadelphia's residents document their suffering over social inequity and socioeconomic strife. The walls simply scream out their wish to document what feels wrong in a city that wreaks of oppression and racial strife.

48. The Health of Trans People

There is clearly a large and public debate about how the transgender community should be treated by society. By engaging in a dialogue about the use of bathrooms, we are publicly debating the basic human rights of the trans community. This fact is horrifying. It is also emblematic of the deep, complex issues in the trans community that are being squelched by policy debates being had by everyone but those who are suffering themselves.

As social workers, we are mandated to have a high level of competency when working with any marginalized community. Given the ways in which trans people are being particularly targeted at this time, our mandate grows considerably. Here are some ways to enhance our work with trans people, to lessen the burden of the persecution that continues to doggedly follow this diverse treatment population.

First, language matters. It matters a lot. That is important to know, because using precise and inclusive language is an intervention unto itself. The best way to talk about the trans community, at this moment in time, is to simply use the word *TRANS*. *Transgendered* and *transgender* don't quite represent the intricacies of the community. The word *transgendered* suggests that there is a clear and discrete migration between gender identities that has a beginning, middle, and end. This is rarely the case. Although some do officially transition, the process of transitioning may be to a non-binary identity or may be experienced as nonlinear. Transitioning is rather intricate and lacks the simple directionality that the word *transgendered* suggests. The term *transgender* is preferable, but it is still not properly inclusive. This is because it is based, still, on a binary gender system that suggests that travel exists between genders, rather than landing on a genderqueer, or nonconforming, identity.

Second, the terms F (female) to M (male) or M (male) to F (female) are no longer suitable descriptors of the process of identifying as trans. First, the terms suggest that one was ever definitively male or definitely female. Instead, we now say AFAB (assigned female at birth) or AMAB (assigned male at birth). This means that because of the presentation of specific genitalia at birth, a gender was assigned. However, this gender is often a misassignment based on biological markers. The assumption that biological markers signify a specific gender identity is problematic, and it is what has led to the suffering of so many. To say that one's presumed gender identity was a byproduct of an assumption, but not a felt identity, is the best way to conceptualize the trans experience.

While we have moved into a space, hopefully, of asking people what their "preferred gender pronoun" is, that language also falls short. The term *preferred* suggests that this is optional for people and simply something that they are selecting by choice. The pronoun that someone uses is not a preference, but a fact of their identity. When we mis-pronoun someone or use the term *preferred,* we are engaged in a microaggression that leaves our trans clients feeling unseen and misunderstood.

As social workers, as we look toward becoming supportive allies of the trans community, we need to truly interrogate what it means to be an ally. As professionals who engage at all with diagnosis or even consult with the *DSM,* we are engaged in a system that oppresses the trans community. By being members of the mental health community, we are assigned a role in the medical treatment of the trans community. Many medical providers will not provide gender confirmation interventions (I am not saying gender reassignment, please note, because we are confirming authentic gender experiences, not reassigning gender) without the approval of a mental health professional.

> **Language matters. It matters a lot. That is important to know, because using precise and inclusive language is an intervention unto itself.**

The World Professional Association for Transgender Health (WPATH) suggests that medical intervention should be preceded by the documented presence of well documented gender dysphoria, capacity for consent to treatment, and "well controlled" mental health. This puts us, as mental health providers, in the tricky position of gatekeeping for a population that ought to be treated as experts on their own lives. Furthermore, the suggestion that mental health suffering ought to be relieved before medical intervention confounds a lot of what we have come to know about how taxing it is to subsume an authentic identity.

If we cannot properly examine the way in which social work has been indoctrinated into a complex set of power dynamics, which often disenfranchise the trans population, then we can't truly assume our role as competent practitioners. We are part of the machine that feels entitled to legislate what public restroom someone uses, despite the fact that we feel so removed from that specific debate.

Trans people are struggling to assert their most basic human rights. The fact is that no one feels comfortable using public bathrooms. The act of using one is inherently anxiety provoking for a host of both obvious and more subtle reasons. The fact that someone would have to enter this already uncomfortable situation with an additional fear of being either found out or misgendered highlights the very precarious position that trans people are in at this exact sociocultural moment in time.

49. The Mental Health of Trans People

There is no one way to ever practice with a specific population. There are typically themes that are worth making note of as we engage in clinical work, though. For example, no two eating disorder clients are the same. But the fact that treatment typically takes eight years when working with anorexia certainly does inform one's thinking. The same is true when working with the trans population. There is huge diversity within the trans population, and the term *trans* is merely an umbrella term. Nonetheless, there are certain clinical themes and concepts that are worthy of our engagement when cultivating a set of best practices.

It is essential to note that the idea of transitioning occurs on a continuum. While some people are migrating from the gender that they were assigned at birth to becoming male or female identified, others are not on a journey with a clear beginning, middle, and end. There are many trans people who identify with the gender that they were assigned at birth while performing other gender identities only some of the time. There are others who are gender queer or non-binary who are not identifying with either traditional gender, male or female. We have been left with a social construct, largely perpetuated by people like Caitlin Jenner and Chaz Bono, which suggests that transitioning is a one-way process. This, in fact, is not always the case. The process of transitioning cannot be reduced as a linear movement from point A to point B.

For many trans individuals, the wish to use hormone replacement therapy (HRT) is a central piece of their transition. This triangulates social workers, leaving us in the role of agents of social control. To use health insurance to cover the HRT, a mental health professional must become involved to give an assessment. This has created tense and problematic relationships, many times, between the trans community and the mental health community. This tension is completely legitimate and ought to be recognized by the clinician. To be placed in the role of gatekeeper of someone's gender transition process almost inevitably places the client in a "down" position within a complex power structure. It is also worth noting that because of the need for health insurance, there is a socioeconomic dimension added to this power structure. Clients with more privilege, and less of a need to use health insurance, are less likely to be embroiled in mental health treatment as permission giver. Certainly, this threatens the possibility of creating a safe space to do clinical work, and extra care must be taken to assure this safety.

Of course, not all people who transition use HRT. Some opt for surgery, and others opt out of any medical intervention at all. It has been found that medical intervention often lessens the distress of feeling wrongly gendered, providing individuals with the relief of creating a body that feels more like home. Although there are mental health issues that are associated with being trans, medical intervention often alleviates these issues alone. Having "top surgery" or removing one's Adam's apple can provide more psychological relief than any social work ever could. We must maintain a dual eye on the work we can do and the limits of our field in working to relieve feelings of gender inauthenticity.

For some, the wish to transition has been a long-standing wish— something that they have been aware of since early childhood. For others, the notion of transitioning came at them in a fast and furious manner. Neither internal experience is more or less valid than the other. There is a faulty, and largely shared, assumption that the longer one has suffered in the "closet," the more legitimate their experience of gender dysphoria is. In fact, all we know about those who have suffered longer than others is that some have seen others transition and are aware of the possibility, and others may have never even been exposed to the option. The other interpretation that is worth considering is that different experiences with the closet reveal different internal defensive structures and correlating levels of consciousness.

When working with someone who has a trans identity, it probably is most important to remain aware of the extent to which they walk through the world and that this world is typically a very hostile environment. Leslie Feinberg (1999) wrote about this experience in the book *Trans Liberation: Beyond Pink or Blue*. Feinberg stated, "We live under the constant threat of horrifying violence. We have to worry about what bathroom to use when our bladders are aching. We are forced to consider whether we'll be dragged out of a bathroom and arrested or face a fist fight while our bladders are still aching. It's an everyday reality for us. Human beings must use toilets.... If I go into the women's bathroom, am I prepared for the shouting and shaming? Will someone call security or the cops? If I use the men's room, am I willing to fight my way out? Am I really ready for the violence that could ensue?" (p. 68-69)

This is a striking quote, given that almost two decades later, a lot has changed and a lot certainly has not. Clinically, it can be seductive to enter the fantasy that trans people are living in an increasingly more supportive and open world. This is a dangerous fantasy that might disavow the truth of the trans struggle. Not every trans person struggles equally, and some are more in danger than others. For example, the more that someone "passes," the safer they are. Or, being a White trans person often lends a layer of safety that trans people of color do not have. In fact, the National Coalition of Anti-Violence Programs found that 40 percent of the fatal attacks against the lesbian, gay, bisexual, and transgender (LGBT) community in 2011 specifically targeted trans women, particularly trans women of color.

Successful work with trans people requires a deft awareness of several issues. We must remain aware of our power, which can be exploitive, when working with the trans population. We also must remain aware of the idiosyncratic nature of each client's transition process. We must be aware of the intrapsychic reverberations of a national debate about bathrooms, which is a debate about human dignity and human rights. And lastly, and perhaps most importantly, we must sustain a rich awareness of the ways in which intersecting identities increase vulnerability and invisibility in nearly equal measure.

50. What Really Triggers Us

The use or overuse of the word *trigger* has become so prevalent that the significance of the word has diminished greatly. You might read a blog post that offers a trigger warning, a professor might offer a trigger warning at the beginning of a class, or you might hear people using the word *triggered* to describe how they are feeling in response to the current political climate. These trigger warnings and utterances are being used to describe a wide array of psychological states, often leaving us confused about what the word means. The fact is that being triggered is a very specific psychological state, and understanding its precise presentation is quite valuable.

First, it is important to know that being triggered is about having first been *traumatized*. The word *triggered* signifies that a trauma has occurred and that specific stimuli can bring us back to this traumatized state. It is understood that the impact of trauma is stored in both the brain and the body. In the brain, it can be stored in the form of flashbacks, reluctance around attachment, and a confused sense of self-worth. In the body, it can be stored as cortisol, a stress hormone that courses through the body and can feel like poison as it runs through us. It can also be stored as a heightened sense of vigilance, as we move rapidly between flight and fight states.

Trauma is based on our inability to make sense of what is happening to us. The process of metabolizing trauma takes an incredible amount of time and is often unending. As we try and sort through it, or to deny it, pieces of our traumatic experience break off and rest in us both physically and psychologically. But because we are driven to make sense of our lives and our worlds, the traumatic material cannot remain in an interminably resting state.

Triggers, external stimuli in our environment, awaken our more traumatized states and leave us feeling both fragile and raw. However, there are a few serious misconceptions about triggers. First, triggers don't exist as literally as we think they do. For example, if there is a student in a class who has faced a horrible history of racial oppression, a professor might offer a trigger warning to help that student prepare for viewing a movie about slavery. There is an assumption that material that feels close to the originally traumatizing material will be experienced as triggering. Although this is somewhat true, it doesn't actually capture the way the whole process evolves. We are, instead, actually traumatized by more subtle cues and unconscious communications.

So, the movie about slavery would likely be experienced as traumatizing if everyone watching it disavowed the tragedy of it, expressed denial about it, watched it without affect, or was able to move on to another topic seamlessly. See, we are actually most triggered by being exposed to the defenses used to negotiate our original trauma rather than by the actual material that we are watching or hearing about. We are also triggered by witnessing or experiencing affective states that bring us back to our original trauma. Because trauma is not something that we can really make sense of cognitively, it lives in us in a more primitive way than that. We almost sense the danger of it with instincts, not thoughts. These instincts are evoked by seeing the same signs of danger that we have originally been unable to manage. But the signs of danger are usually forms of communication and interaction, not literal words or images.

I was recently in a session when I closed my eyes to picture what a client was describing. It was for a mere second or two. We were not talking about anything particularly charged. However, in this moment, my client described an immediate feeling of being triggered. Her abuser often closed his eyes when yelling at her. His closed eyes were a sign of danger to her. My closed eyes were a sign of danger to her, leaving her feeling as if she was in an aroused and heightened state.

This heightened state is one that can last anywhere from a few minutes to a few weeks. People usually don't stay triggered for more than two weeks, because the mind starts to re-regulate and store the trauma in more distant recesses of the mind. However, there are some settings that make the ceasing of the triggered state more unlikely. If external stimuli constantly signify danger, the feeling of being triggered will sustain. If family members constantly remain in a state of denial or disavowal, this will allow being triggered to remain. Further, our clients typically feel the most ashamed, which is a feeling that accompanies any trauma, if they feel triggered by events that happened a long time ago. It is important, in these instances, to remind our clients that the unconscious—where trauma is most powerfully stored—has no sense of time, and the passage of more or less time really doesn't change much at all.

> **The unconscious— where trauma is most powerfully stored—has no sense of time.**

Being triggered is very real, but it also actually means something specific and powerful. The overuse of the term cheapens the gravity of the triggered state. It also keeps us from studying the ways in which a triggered state can be properly nurtured. The main intervention for feeling triggered is the reduction of external stimuli. This means less noise, less screen time, less talking in large groups, and less offering up of ourselves to help others understand our internal world. The more that we are able to find peace, quiet, trusting relationships, and the presence of others who understand us, the less metastatic the trigger. The more we are able to recognize the need to tend to our own rawness, living in us like a sunburn, the less likely we are to leave ourselves out and unprotected for more searing.

51. When Everything Hurts

I am not writing this with the assumption that everyone feels the same way about the outcome of the 2016 election. At the same time, I am sure that we share in the reality of the fact that our country feels deeply divided. Our clients are suffering because of this. Many of our clients, of course, have been suffering for decades, and the outcome of an election doesn't change a thing. But, for me, the election has highlighted some stark truths that have shifted my clinical practice. These are some of my realizations.

We can no longer subscribe to a binary between micro and macro practice.

In social work school, we are asked to select a "track" and to refine our area of study very early on. These decisions likely guide our course selections and placements for the two years of our time in school. They also place us in silos that prevent us from truly studying the constant interplay between the field and the world, the treatment room and the street, the Affordable Care Act and the clinical hour.

As policy inevitably will change over the next four years, our clients' lives will inevitably be affected. It is going to be essential to stay on top of how policy shifts and to work to prepare our clients for these changes. Sitting with them in the pain and the disappointment of policy changes will not suffice. We need to also serve as their eyes and ears as services rapidly shift and entitlements dissipate.

We also need to become even more aware of the ways in which policy is currently having an impact on our clients' lives, presidential politics or not. This is because the outcome of the election was essentially a desperate cry out for change. Although I am not sure of the change we will get, I do know that the status quo was already leaving huge parts of our population behind, and this is not something to which we can continue to remain blind.

The economy is a social justice issue. The economy is a clinical issue.

While we are tempted to think about the use of social services as highly correlated with unemployment, it is actually the working poor in this country who are suffering tremendously. Walmart employs 1%

of the American working population and is the largest private American employer. Their employees are heavily subsidized by the public because of low wages and benefits. Many employees work up to 60 hours a week and are still not able to put food on their tables.

There is no way to think of that as simply an issue of economic inequality, although of course it is. It is also an issue of psychological suffering. As social workers, we need to think in wholes, not parts. When we hear about shocking economic disparity, much of which we suffer from ourselves, we are the ones who need to listen for the interplay between the mind and the environment, the mind and systemic oppression, the mind and the shame of never having enough.

Trauma is awoken in the ways that we don't always understand.

For my clients with histories of sexual assault, the results of this election have been electrifyingly painful. The fact that the candidate elected had been implicated in past sexual misconduct made several of my clients feel that their perpetrators had been vindicated. I have had clients share feelings of being locked in a room with their perpetrators, while others have discussed a wish to move into a cabin in the woods to feel safe.

The wish for safety has never felt more pronounced in my work. And my inability to clearly offer it has never felt more difficult. I don't necessarily think this is a *bad* thing. Instead, I think it is just a *real* thing. There are painful psychological states that we can bear witness to and survive with our clients, but it isn't our job to fix it. And the surrender to our inability to "fix it" can only deepen our work.

We don't know what we don't know.

I spent the first week after the 2016 national election watching my clients watch me for some sort of answer or relief. I spent it listening to my clients listening for my reassurance that things are going to be okay. The fact is that I don't know any more about the future than my clients do. And I never have. But sometimes I feel like I do, and this is an inauthentic performance on my part. I have worked diligently to not reassure beyond that which I am capable. I have also worked alongside, not ahead of, my clients in their efforts to make meaning and sense of how the world is changing around us. And I do believe that meaning can and will be made, together.

A movement is unfolding.

I have never seen so many of my peers become activated in such a short amount of time. Nearly everyone I know has become increasingly informed and moved toward action. If this movement is going to work, social workers MUST be a part of it. I know we are overworked, and I know that our work is already activism. At the same time, our systemic view of the world and our capacity to hold intersectionality is what will make this movement sustainable. I have never believed in the wisdom of social workers and psychological thought more than I do now. It is our time to demand a seat at the table, as we see how our clients' rights fade and the coverage for the work that we do evaporates.

It is always darkest before the dawn.

I was sitting on the floor of my kitchen at work because we were out of seats the other day, and I made a joke about feeling like the kitchen was a bomb shelter. Everyone laughed and agreed that the safety of this small room of social workers was indeed a bomb shelter. In reflecting on this, I realized that with the comfort and direction toward the future that we must find, we must find in our own experience, our own camaraderie, and our own practice wisdom.

It is only through the support of other social workers that the ways forward will be lit. I am going to try and shine a little light. I hope you do, too.

Sunset

Sunsets are worthy of obsession. There are never two sunsets that look alike, and they are offered to us daily. If you can't catch a sunset at 4:30 p.m. in the winter, it will set at 6:00 p.m. toward springtime. In the summer, you have until almost 9:00 p.m. And there is no color that a sunset can offer that doesn't somehow seem to soothe a different piece of the soul.

52. An Internal Home for the Holidays

Although not everyone agrees on how the results of the election feel, the fact is that the majority of my clients have been seriously suffering. In fact, in more than a decade of practicing, I have never seen anything quite like what I am seeing right now. Session after session, my clients are coming in with feelings of complete despair and hopelessness. I work with a very marginalized population, most of whom are afraid for the future of their civil rights, their health insurance, and their overall safety in the world. And the fact is that I am running out of things to say. This is partly because I feel similar to how they do. It is also because I feel as if we are in some uncharted territory, societally, where the rules of how we typically think things function don't seem to apply. We are in a new era with a murky future. Our ability to make sense of things feels different. And, the ways to navigate through it are certainly not obvious.

I have been repeatedly asking myself, *what is it that I am doing, anyway?* I don't know any more than my clients know about how things are going to turn out. All I have is my training, my colleagues, and my ability to reflect. All of these have been falling short for me in some ways. But in the past few days, I have started to recalibrate a bit, to find an increased clarity about my purpose.

This clarity came to me when imagining going home for Thanksgiving. I am not sure who feels that Thanksgiving is simple, but I am not one of those people. Neither are most of my clients. I generally find that the return home can unleash a tremendous amount of fear and regression. After all, we walk around with a snapshot of what is available to us during these family traditions, and it leaves us with information that we negotiate throughout the year. We feel crowded out at the table or that there is a seat for us; we feel that there are enough resources or that there is a scarcity; we feel that someone remembered that we are a vegetarian and made us a special meal or we feel invisible when there is nothing to eat. Thanksgiving themes end up being life themes, and during the actual holiday, these themes are experienced as intense realities.

Struggling with my own feelings about returning home, I remembered a bit about why we do this work. I went into my own mind and soothed myself with some important pieces of information:

- I knew I would probably overeat, because I can become socially anxious and use food to comfort this.

- I knew that there would be a lot of small talk that would be difficult for me to negotiate, because I am fairly introverted and prefer deep conversations.

- I knew that no matter how I felt during the meal, that the feelings would pass and I would be cozy at home soon enough.

- I knew that even though my family really loves me, they still say incredibly hurtful things and this has more to do with them than it does with me.

- I knew that the opportunity to be together is still an opportunity, even if it brings complicated feelings with it.

These thoughts, musings, and feelings are pieces of my internal world. And because of my relationship with myself, my loved ones, my therapist, my supervisor, my colleagues, and my clients, I can enter this internal world and find comfort and wisdom. And so I recalled, that amidst the election fear and turmoil, and amidst the holiday parades, that our work as clinical social workers remains steady to assist in the *solid development of soothing internal worlds*.

There have been times of strife before this election—much worse strife, in fact. And there will be times of strife in the future. Our work, always, is to help clients have in them inner mechanisms that prepare them for this strife. There are several elements that help clients to develop inner worlds that soothe anxiety, depression, and fear.

First, it is essential to remind ourselves and our clients that we are not working to eliminate painful affect states. Instead, we are working to find the tools to survive the inevitability of these states, with the assurance that there are feelings of relief that almost always come with time and connection.

It is also essential to remember that by sitting quietly with clients and offering them our complete focus and curiosity, we are aiding them in the process of taking in that quiet and curiosity and starting the construction of that very real estate within their own minds. The simple act of setting aside a sacred frame for our work translates into the possibility of having this infrastructure within us. Further, by bearing witness to our clients' affect states that feel intolerable and not becoming swept up in their storms, we remind them that their internal experiences can be survived with both feet on the ground.

In addition to bearing witness, we also help our clients in the process of growing insight about what is going on with them. By paying close attention to their patterns of behavior, of thought, of self-sabotage, of dreams, and of realities, we see and learn things that are blind spots for our clients. By gently sharing these observations, we invite clients into the study of their own minds. As students of their own psyches, they begin to gain a certain mastery over their own behaviors, even as they remain somewhat enslaved by them. Take, for example, my very unoriginal overeating at Thanksgiving. I haven't mastered it, but I do understand it, and that understanding helps ease my own fears about losing control.

I have been doing a lot of thinking about Anne Frank recently. I specifically reflected on her use of her diary. Her diary was a place for her to export her internal world and to then have her internal world reflected back to her. She was able to make use of this tool, the tool of her own mind, to survive and comfort herself through horrifying conditions and daily fear and terror. I think this was largely made possible by the security of her family connections—connections that were good and loving. She was able to sustain the sentiment that, "Despite everything, I believe that people are really good at heart."

It is useful to remember that there are many different parts we can play in the Anne Frank story. We can be the secure attachment that made her good faith possible. We can be the actual diary that reflects the realities of one's inner world. We can be the reader of the diary sharing what we see as the story unfolds. Or we can sit, side by side, as the storms pass through—mutually unsure of the outcome—but mutually assured of the importance of being together, so that being alone won't hurt as much when that time comes.

53. Social Work as Moral Compass

A year ago, the world felt like a much different place. I am not entirely sure that it was, but it certainly felt like it. Since the 2016 national election, a feeling of uncertainty has pervaded so many different realms, including everything from health insurance to international policy. Amidst these uncharted waters, social work is not only a ship worth sailing on, but one that might help us all find some sort of shore.

I sit down many mornings nearly paralyzed by the devastating level of needs in our country and abroad. Whether it is the insufficient comfort brought by a full-time minimum wage job or the intensifying and seemingly unending refugee crisis occurring because of the war on Syrian citizens, trauma and injustice abound. I wonder if I should turn toward the news or turn away from it. I wonder what news sources I can even trust. I feel the urge to numb out with capitalist tools, like using my Target Red Card for a 5% discount or ordering extra appetizers at some national chain restaurant.

Then I head to work and have a day of clients ahead of me and remind myself that this is where the cure to these desperate feelings lies. Amidst poverty, war, disenfranchised voters—a theme emerges. The suffering comes down to a few unifying factors—trauma, ruptured attachment, and developmental misattunement. These factors elevate the utmost importance of our work, which is to be with someone who is suffering, in an open, containing, thoughtful, intimate, and tender way.

In his quest to determine how to best treat those suffering after World War II, Carl Jung (1933) wrote, "The shoe that fits one person pinches another; there is no recipe for living that suits all cases." Here, Jung captures the ways in which our work differs from so many other fields. We sit with clients in the service of honoring their idiosyncrasies. We study their attachment patterns, meditate on how their traumatic past is making itself known in the present, and adjust our treatment to honor the truth of their psychological age, rather than their chronological age.

And in response to our studies, we create ways of being, ways of using our selves differentially and create interventions. We know that these interventions don't come easily, and we know that they don't always work. We test hypotheses about their usefulness before even implementing them. For example, if we have an addicted client, we don't say, "Go to a 12-step meeting!" Instead, we ask, "Do you feel like you are ready to go to a 12-step meeting?" or "Can you imagine that a 12-step meeting might feel useful right now?" We collaborate before forcing solutions, and we respect stages of readiness before moving forward.

> **When we provide individuals with the space to think, to broaden their emotional literacy, to feel what feels un-feelable, we send change agents out into the world.**

When we, as social workers, sit with clients, we recognize the truly healing capacity of simple curiosity and attention to detail. If a client tells us that they have a performance this week that they are nervous about, we know how curative it is to remember this the following week and to ask about it. We know that one of the keys to creating internal change in a client's mind is our ability to demonstrate that they are worthy of being internalized, being remembered, being thought about. We know that the selves of clients are brought to life by our willingness to hold their lives in our minds.

We also know that to talk is to heal. We don't exactly know why, but the edict holds that once something is said out loud, it loses its psychological power. We are in the business of the "talking cure," Freud's original idea, which is based on helping others experience the neurobiological relief of connection via verbalization of otherwise seemingly unsayable truths. J. Gary Sparks (2007) wrote in his book, *At the Heart of Matter,* that, "It is addressing life in the present that cleanses and heals a festering wound." We cleanse wounds through tender psychological touch and exploration. We don't rush our questions, but we don't shy away from the hard ones either. We allow our clients' cues to pace our inquiry, without necessarily letting our clients' defenses control us either.

And, most of all, we know that we are in the business of enriching one's own conversation with oneself. The true fruit of clinical social work's labor is the enriching of internal psychic lives. Jung, after diligently studying the etiology of the events of WWII, particularly the psyche of the German people before Hitler's ascension to power, felt that there had been a loss of focus on the value of inner life. He found that imagination had become deadened in the face of increasing complacency and surrender to multiple status quos. To ward off this complacency, we need to work with our clients to heighten their level of consciousness and ward off levels of destructive unconsciousness. The more our world falls prey to the unconscious forces that perpetuate inequality, hatred, and oppression, the more intense our vulnerability is to neglecting each other.

However, consciousness—the kind that is born out of the intimacy of the clinical dyad—creates, radiates, and metastasizes actual change. Change for the individual, change for a family, change for a work place, change for the world. When we provide individuals with the space to think, to broaden their emotional literacy, to feel what feels *un-feelable,* we send change agents out into the world—agents ready to share these morally just acts of interpersonal love and relatedness.

References

American Academy of Pediatrics. (2016). Poverty and child health in the United States. Retrieved from *http://pediatrics.aappublications. org/content/early/2016/03/07/peds.2016-0339*

Benjamin, J. (2004). Beyond doer and done to: An intersubjective view of thirdness. *Psychoanalytic Quarterly, 73,* 5-46.

Clance, P. R., & Imes, S. A. (1978). The impostor phenomenon in high achieving women: Dynamics and therapeutic intervention. *Psychotherapy: Theory, Research, and Practice, 15,* 241-247.

Coates, S., Schechter, D., & Rosenthal, J. (2003). *Brief interventions with traumatized children and families after September 11: Trauma and human bonds* (pp. 23-49). New York, NY: The Analytic Press/Taylor & Francis Group.

Feinberg, L. (1999). *Trans liberation: Beyond pink or blue.* Boston, MA: Beacon Press.

Ferenczi, S. (1919). On the technique of psycho-analysis. In: *Further contributions to the theory and technique of psycho-analysis.* Hogarth Press, 1950.

Fisher, K. A. (1970). The iconoclast's notebook. *Psychotherapy: Theory, Research, Practice, Training, 7,* 54-56.

Jung, C. (1933). *Modern man in search of a soul.* London, England: Kegan Paul, Trench, Trubner and Company.

Miller, A. (1981). *The drama of the gifted child.* New York, NY: Basic Books.

National Association of Social Workers (NASW). (2008). *Code of Ethics.* Washington, DC: Author. Retrieved from *http://www.naswdc.org*

Ogden, T. (1994). The analytic third: Working with intersubjective clinical facts. *International Journal of Psycho-Analysis, 75,* 3-20.

Pennsylvania Department of Human Services. (2015). Annual child abuse report—2014. Retrieved from *http://www.dhs.pa.gov/cs/groups/webcontent/documents/report/c_208256.pdf*

Perez-Pena, R. (2015, September 21). 1 in 4 women experience sex assault on campus. *The New York Times.*

Pierce, M. (2006). Intergenerational transmission of trauma: What have we learned from our work. *International Journal of Psychoanalysis, 87,* 555-557.

Singer, J. B. (Producer). (2015, November 2). #99 — Becoming a clinical social worker: Interview with Dr. Danna Bodenheimer [Audio Podcast]. *Social Work Podcast.* Retrieved from *http://www.socialworkpodcast.com/2015/11/Bodenheimer.html*

Sparks, J. G. (2007). *At the heart of matter: Syncronicity and Jung's spiritual testament.* Toronto, Canada: Inner City Books.

Starecheski, L. (2015). Take the ACE quiz and learn what it does and doesn't mean. NPR. Retrieved from *http://www.npr.org/sections/health-shots/2015/03/02/387007941/take-the-ace-quiz-and-learn-what-it-does-and-doesnt-mean*

Tosone, C., Bettman, J., Minami, T., & Jasperson, R. (2010). New York City social workers after 9/11: Their attachment, resiliency, and compassion fatigue. *International Journal of Emergency Mental Health, 12*(2),103-16.

Yalom, I. (1981). *Existential psychotherapy.* New York, NY: Basic Books.

Young-Bruehl, E. (2012). *Childism: Confronting prejudice against children.* New Haven, CT: Yale University Press.

About the Author

Dr. Danna Bodenheimer, LCSW, lives and works in Philadelphia, PA. She received both her bachelor's and master's degrees from Smith College, in addition to attending a post-baccalaureate program in psychology at Columbia University. Danna went on to receive her doctorate in social work from the University of Pennsylvania.

Danna divides her time between consulting, supervising, writing, and practicing. After nearly 10 years in private practice, Danna opened the Walnut Psychotherapy Center, an outpatient, trauma-informed mental health practice that serves the LGBTQ population. The practice makes use of psychodynamic therapy and strives to make long-term mental health treatment affordable and available to as many people in Philadelphia as possible.

Danna has taught at the University of Pennsylvania, Temple University, Rutgers University, and currently at Bryn Mawr's Graduate School of Social Work and Social Research. She teaches clinical practice and classes on gender and sexuality. Danna is now the head of the Walnut Psychotherapy Center.

She is the mother of two fascinating and inquisitive young boys. She uses social work theory to understand both her personal life and her professional life, strongly believing that social work is the field that will lead us forward into a more equitable and just future. Using Philadelphia as a landscape to study issues of oppression, intersecting identities, and complex socioeconomic struggle, Danna's love of and commitment to social work deepens steadily over time.

Danna received the 2011-2012 Award for Excellence in Teaching from the University of Pennsylvania. She was also selected as a fellow for the American Psychoanalytic Association for 2012-2013. She is a licensed clinical social worker (LCSW) in Pennsylvania.

Follow Danna's writing at *http://www.socialworker.com/dannab* and photography on Instagram at *@phillyviewed*.

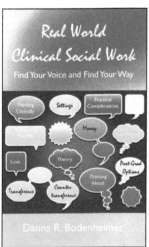

Social Work Titles Published by White Hat Communications/ The New Social Worker Press

On Clinical Social Work: Meditations and Truths From the Field
The A-to-Z Self-Care Handbook for Social Workers
and Other Helping Professionals
Real World Clinical Social Work
Days in the Lives of Social Workers
More Days in the Lives of Social Workers
Days in the Lives of Gerontological Social Workers
Riding the Mutual Aid Bus and Other Adventures in Group Work
Beginnings, Middles, & Ends: Sideways Stories
on the Art and Soul of Social Work
Is It Ethical?
The Field Placement Survival Guide
The New Social Worker Magazine

Visit us online at:

The New Social Worker Online
http://www.socialworker.com

SocialWorkJobBank
http://www.socialworkjobbank.com

White Hat Communications Store
http://shop.whitehatcommunications.com

Network with us:

http://www.facebook.com/newsocialworker
http://www.facebook.com/socialworkjobbank
http://www.facebook.com/realworldcsw
http://www.twitter.com/newsocialworker
https://www.linkedin.com/groups/3041069
https://plus.google.com/+Socialworkermag